Annual 2007

TEXT PUBLISHING
MELBOURNE AUSTRALIA

The Text Publishing Company
Swann House
22 William Street
Melbourne Victoria 3000
Australia
www.textpublishing.com.au

Most of the articles in *The Chaser Annual* were first published in *The Chaser* online at www.chaser.com.au
This edition published in 2007 by The Text Publishing Company

Designed and typeset by Roxy Gilbey
Cover by Peter Long. Back cover image by Fiona Katauskas.
Printed in Australia by BPA Print Group

ISBN 978-1-921351-08-2
ISSN 1445-9094

Contents

Contributors

Writers
Richard Cooke
Shane Cubis
Dominic Knight
Chas Licciardello
Julian Morrow
Craig Reucassel

Additional material
Scott Dooley
Lisa Pryor
David Stewart
Gregor Stronach
Chris Taylor

Cartoonists
Fiona Katauskas
Andrew Weldon

Design and layout
Roxy Gilbey

Chaser administration
Siân Dyce

Introduction

Welcome to the eighth instalment of *The Chaser Annual*. While in 2007 The Chaser's name became known to a wider audience thanks to the inexplicable popularity of *The War on Everything*, we are proud to be able to show a much smaller number of people why, in the years before the television show, The Chaser was largely unknown for its mildly amusing, largely lame pun-based news satire.

2007 was the year Australia hosted APEC, of course. Never before have so many dignitaries gathered together to achieve so little, other than at the UN. The 21 world leaders issued a Sydney Declaration on climate change, which was a remarkable testament to the APEC leaders' shared willingness to take meaningful steps to avoid binding targets.

Because our own involvement in the event is still before the courts, we are unfortunately unable to write anything more about the APEC meeting, other than that Chas and Jules are guilty as sin, and that we would like the court to take this helpful denouncement into account in determining any future sentences for other members of the team.

This has been a year of high-profile retirements. Shane Warne said farewell from the Test team this year, which was bad news for our cricket team and worse news for our two-bit comedians. Relief came only in late August, with the revelations about Andrew Johns' drug-taking. The news was a particular boon for the NRL *Footy Show*, which not only brokered a tell-all interview but expressed interest in signing the "manic" half of his personality to appear in comedy sketches.

Queensland and Victoria also saw the retirements of popular, charismatic premiers, while NSW was stuck with its unpopular, bland premier for another four years. This year also marks the retirement of John Laws, whose remarkable broadcasting legacy will inspire future generations of broadcasters to comply with the cash-for-comments rules. Other departures included Luciano Pavarotti, who went to a better place, and Mohamed Haneef, who thought he'd come to a better place, was proven horribly wrong, and has now escaped to a country with a civilised legal system – India.

We did, however, welcome home another person who the government assures us is a terrorist despite never having had a proper trial. David Hicks was brought back to Adelaide, and immediately regretted leaving the comforts of Gitmo. This brilliant political move by the Government deprived the Left of its favorite excuse for a rally, leaving them to protest only about WorkChoices, Iraq, APEC, Burma, and climate change. This year's trendiest bourgeois cause reached its somewhat underwhelming climax at Live Earth. Never before has an event designed to combat global warming consumed so much electricity.

But the biggest story this year, of course, has been the election. After a shockingly soporific decade, this was the year Australian politics became slightly less tedious again. And on that note, we would like to bid a fond farewell to Kim Beazley, whose greatest contribution to our public life was the blissful few years he allowed the nation to devote its attention elsewhere. With his departure from the leadership, though, it has been interesting to watch as the nation became disillusioned with John Howard. If this wasn't surprising enough, voters' apparent lack of disillusionment with Kevin Rudd has been nothing short of remarkable.

When this book hits the streets (and we mean literally the streets, and more specifically the gutters) we will be on the verge of a Federal election. And despite the positive polls for Labor, by mid-November we will probably be staring down the barrel of another Howard victory. It is surely only moments until ASIO unmasks a last-minute plot by Muslim refugee terrorists who threaten to increase interest rates by throwing themselves overboard.

Still, for much of the year, politics has been a genuine contest, the likes of which we haven't seen since Mark Latham fought that compelling battle against his own demons.

By the time the next election *Annual* rolls around in 2010, though (in the unlikely event our careers last that long) we now know that John Howard will no longer be Prime Minister, whether by his own hand or that of Kevin Rudd. The Chaser has never existed without John Howard in the top job, so his departure will take some getting used to. But we are confident that we will be provided with rich satirical fodder by Kevin Rudd – much of it in Mandarin – and his Liberal counterpart, whoever that may be after Peter Costello is quickly dumped. Otherwise, Australians risk being governed with competence. Fortunately for the nation's satirists, we can be assured that will never happen.

Sydney prepares for second ever day of supporting Swans

With fair-weather conditions expected for the Grand Final, Sydney will again be awash with mint-condition guernseys, as the city rechristens the Swans "we" for 48 hours. Beer gardens more accustomed to the clink of cocktail glasses and the mild groove of chill-out compilations will soon resound with cries of "ball", shouted half-a-second behind the crowd at the ground.

Sometime Swannies fan Jim Stewart will be one of those there in the thick of it, applauding every behind. He may have missed every home game since the Swans moved to Sydney in 1982, but he's already wearing his scarf, which smells faintly of mothballs.

"I can't wait until kick-off,"

says the twenty-something marketing man, riding high on a wave of forced enthusiasm. "That feeling when the whistle blows, and the game starts – there's nothing else like it on TV."

Stewart will be watching the game at an Eastern suburbs bowling club, a venue he has not been to since last year's Grand Final involving Sydney. Beset by Swans fever, he has spent the past week cribbing key player names from media reports, and plans to drop the three he has managed to remember into conversation on match day.

Stephanie Edwards, 24, will also be a vital member of Stewart's three-quarter-length-pant-wearing coterie on

Swans fans: no sweat, tears or Bloods

game day. "AFL has the hottest guys," she says, a sentiment she last expressed twelve months ago.

Edwards will contribute to the festival atmosphere by asking whether Warwick Capper still plays for Sydney, a suggestion that will be scathingly mocked by male members of her party, several of whom believe Paul Kelly and Tony Lockett still play for the team. She will then lose interest in the game

half way through the second quarter. But until that moment arrives, she's as one-eyed as they come. "Go Swannies," she shouts, for the tenth time in as many minutes.

Asked about the Swans' chances, the inner-city cheer squad are unanimous. "If the refereeing is good, and Robert Thompson has a good game, then we're going to win the Championship," Stewart says. "Who are we playing again?"

Lazy environmentalist stages drive against global warming

Inspired by the success of the Walk Against Warming event, self-described fan of the environment Juan Martinez is staging a one-man road trip to fight climate change. With a "honk if you hate fossil fuels" bumper sticker firmly in place, Martinez will drive his dilapidated Kombi van on a whistle-stop tour to his local shopping centre, spreading his anti-global warming message to fellow motorists on the way. "Think global, act local," he says.

Martinez says he had intended to participate in the Walk Against Warming, but somehow "never got round to it."

"I started off thinking about a bike-ride, but I'm not in great shape, and it's pretty dangerous with all the cars on the road. Then I thought I'd drive a hybrid car, but

they're pretty pricey," he says. Martinez points out that driving allows him to carry tens of thousands of information booklets printed on high-quality paper.

This is not the first time the semi-committed activist has mounted a campaign of this kind. He once had a team of sky-writers spell out "RATIFY THE KYOTO PROTOCOL NOW" in the skies above Brisbane. But not everyone supports the campaigner's stances.

"People are pretty quick to criticise," he says. "They'll point out that what I'm doing not only harms the environment, but also requires no real effort. But it's often the little things that make a difference. If everyone just left their air-conditioner on full-blast 24-hours a day, temperatures

Martinez prepares for his 7km trek

wouldn't rise as fast. And we can all do our bit for the water crisis by using bottled water whenever we can."

Martinez is now planning a weekend-long lounge-room "stoned sit in" to advocate the decriminalisation of marijuana.

Beazley denies leadership challenge from 'Xavier Rudd'

Beazley addresses the Greens party faithful

Federal Opposition Leader Kim Beazley has rebuffed claims that his leadership might be under challenge, following his embarrassing confusion of Rove McManus and Karl Rove. "I can assure you that I will be leading the ABC to the next election," Beazley announced. "But in any case, Xavier Rudd and I are both utterly devoted to unseating John Howard's government and its extreme agenda."

Beazley later apologised for accidentally thinking of actor John Howard when making his earlier statement.

In the latest Newspoll, which was taken shortly after Beazley's new gaffe, blues and roots musician Xavier Rudd enjoyed a 68% approval as preferred Labor leader over Kim Beazley and Kevin Rudd by virtue of not being either one of them.

Offering his condolences to Karl Rove rather than the newly widowed Rove McManus is the latest in a long line of mental errors for Beazley, the most damaging coming in January 2005 when he erroneously contested for the Labor leadership again.

Beazley immediately put out an apology for the Rove gaffe, claiming that he had "misspoken". However, after further discussions with his caucus colleagues he issued a clarification, instead apologising for having "spoken". However, Rove McManus took the gaffe with good spirits, simply mugging "What the?" to polite but unenthusiastic laughter.

For his part, Karl Rove was delighted to have ended yet another Bush adversary's career, this time without even having to do anything. However, he said he would have been far more pleased if the politician he destroyed had actually been a left-winger.

Tonga asks Australia for security force of its own bouncers

The government of Tonga has called on Australia to restore order in the riot-stricken nation by raising a standing army of Tongan security staff, recruited exclusively from the outside of Australia's pubs and bars. The government hopes the Tongan security force will not only quell the riots, but also prepare the island for national Girls Drink Free day next Friday.

"Our biggest export is doormen," explained Foreign Minister Sonatane Tu'akinamolahi Taumoepeau-Tupou. "The only big burly guys left in the country are not the sort of people you'd let into your pubs, let alone guard them. So you can imagine what happened when they were set loose on our CBD"

Riots broke out last week in protest against the new king's failure to implement democractic reforms to Tonga's constitutional monarchy. "We need a stack of bouncers to help Tonga become a truly modern democracy," the Foreign Minister explained. "But we're not telling the bouncers that of course, because it would only confuse them. We've just told them there's a private party on in the capital and noone gets in unless their name's on the door."

Tonga has asked Australia to send a regular contingent of bouncers as well as a commando squad of lethal "special security forces" recruited from outside the Sydney Casino.

But Prime Minister John Howard may refuse Tonga's request for assistance, as the government is concerned that sending the bouncer security force to Tonga could leave the entries of Australian nitespots with a critical shortage of obnoxious assholes who are predisposed to violence. "If we do what Tonga asks, how will we determine who comes to our nightclubs and the circumstances in which they come?" Mr Howard asked yesterday.

Pacific experts say a Tongan security detachment would ensure than undesirables could not enter the capital Nuku'alofa "unless they're with some really hot girls."

The Government hopes to find nightclub bouncers who have experience with Molotov cocktails

'Bill & Ted' director hoping to jump on threequel bandwagon

The Stallyns before the relentless, crushing realities of life wore them down

Seeking to follow in the footsteps of well-received movies like *Spider-Man 3*, *Shrek the Third* and *Pirates of the Caribbean: At World's End*, director Stephen Herek has announced plans to make *Bill & Ted's Radical Pilgrimage* later this year. "I think the time is right for us to all learn what happened to the dudes 16 years on," he said. "Are they still married to the babes? Are the Wyld Stallyns still together?"

Although the script is yet to be finalised, early reports claim the film will follow the titular characters as they do battle with an evil version of themselves from another dimension, who represent the impotence of the lower middle class male and the pain of lost youth.

"Bill and Ted have lost their way," explained screenwriter Ed Solomon. "They took office jobs to pay the rent while they got the band up and running, and somehow lost track of the 'Be excellent to each other'

ethos that will inspire future generations. It's gonna be up to Rufus [George Carlin] to show the boys that being middle aged doesn't mean they can't party on, dudes."

There is some controversy over the script. "We're not considering *Bogus Journey* to be canon," said Herek, who did not helm the 1991 sequel. "There are new directions we want to take the franchise in, and characters like the Grim Reaper and Station don't really fit that darker, grittier vision. *Radical Pilgrimage* will be more about enduring friendship, thwarted ambition and excellent air guitar solos."

Hollywood insiders have reported that Alex Winter is keen to reprise his role as Bill, but only if Keanu Reeves agrees to be involved in the project. If Reeves chooses not to take part, the filmmakers are considering John Cusack and Edward Norton Jr for the role of Ted.

Manager orders Bindi to deny exploitation claims

Bindi, relieved her name isn't the type of barb that killed her father

Steve Irwin's daughter Bindi has made a series of carefully stage-managed media appearances to refute claims she is being manipulated. "Dad's manager told me to tell you that I'm totally in control," Bindi said at a live press conference, now also available on DVD. "And I really want to get those toys he promised me."

The press conference comes on the eve of a national book tour to promote Bindi's new autobiography, *Steve Irwin Was My Dad: The Bindi Irwin Story*. The autobiography press release says Bindi decided to write the book "spontaneously and completely of her own accord", noting that she was especially keen to finish the project in time for the Christmas market.

The book was written with the help of professional ghostwriters, who described working with the eight-year-old on her autobiography as "easier than doing Shane Warne's."

Bindi has assumed the spotlight because she shares her father's interest in conservation, and especially conservation of the Irwin family fortune. Bindi's five-year-old brother Bob has been less prominent, preferring to focus instead on being a prop in the crocodile enclosure at Australia Zoo.

Since her father's death, *Crocodile Hunter* director John Stainton has become Bindi's chief male role model. "John's like a father to me," she told *Australian Story* recently. "Like Michael Jackson's father."

Child welfare groups are concerned Bindi's media engagements might be the reason she is doing poorly at school. But supporters say the fact she is Steve Irwin's daughter explains her bad grades. They also deny Bindi is being exploited because of Steve's death, pointing out that Bindi was already being exploited before the Crocodile Hunter died.

Hicks finally granted a legal right: to remain silent

Convicted terrorist David Hicks will soon return to Australia under a plea bargain that will see him serve nine months in jail and bar him from commenting on his case. Hicks has been warned that under a variation on the US's famous Miranda Rights, anything he says can be used against him in a non-court of retrospective law.

The chief military prosecutor, Col. Moc Davis, also clarified that Hicks had enjoyed the right to silence throughout his detention, which was afforded him by means of a sound-proof solitary confinement cell.

The sentencing comes after Hicks pleaded guilty, for his life, and that they please just let him sleep. "Let's not forget Hicks has admitted to being an enemy combatant," Davis said. "And if he wasn't an enemy of the United States Government before he went to Guantanamo, he sure is now."

Many suspect the Australian Federal Government of seeking political benefit by trying to silence Hicks until after the Federal election. Hicks is banned from claiming that he was tortured (especially if the claims involve sleep deprivation or water-boarding), and also from criticising WorkChoices legislation.

But Attorney-General Phillip Ruddock has said that he would be permitted certain types of speech. "If he wanted to speak to the *7.30 Report*, and give an interview full of incriminating details that could be used to construct a solid court case against him, that would be fine." Critics say the suggestion rings false, as the Government has no intention of constructing a solid case against Hicks at any time.

Controversial South Australian Democrat Sandra Kanck has suggested that Hicks become a candidate for the Democrats, a move some on the Coalition benches welcomed. "It's one way of making sure no one ever hears from him again," said Ruddock.

The blurry yet incriminating photo that must accompany any mention of Hicks

NEWSPAPER COLUMNISTS

Unfair generalisations never stopped them, so why should they stop us?

Piers: thinking woman's shorthand for "period"

RIGHT WING UNRELENTING: You'd have to be a card-carrying member of the Hitler Youth to legitimately hold some of the opinions these guys do, and I have a sneaking suspicion they actually write their hard-edge drivel so normal people like us can have their blood angried up. There's an almost parodic element to the work – surely no one with the intelligence to shit out a column every day or so could support a government so unequivocally .

LEFT WING FANATIC: If the Right Wing Unrelenting are the enemy, then this is the ally. I guess. It's a tough job, trying to mount a defence against right wing platforms when your only source of journalistic integrity's currently arguing that his

parents should legally own the TV they hired from Radio Rentals three years ago, that no one should look at women as sexual beings, and the sooner we return to a centralised agrarian state the better. People aren't gonna get behind that, dude.

WOLF IN SHEEP'S CLOTHING: The fancy name for a false moderate – the kind of journo whose column you nod along with, thinking they're making sense of the world in which we live, and then BAM! Suddenly they're advocating the death penalty for civil disobedience and outlining a plan in which all junkies are bussed out to central Australia to fend for themselves.

"FREE THE THIRD WORLD! EAT THE RICH!"

MEN ARE FROM MARS, MY KITTEN'S FROM VENUS *MEOW*: Where's the justice in a world that allows people to earn a comfortable living from masturbation? I'm not talking about those hot, pnuematic porn stars who put on a show for

Adorable. And worth writing 500 words about.

the discerning gentleman. Cutesy tales of suburban homeliness wrought by men and women with the chutzpah to think anyone wants to hear about their mundane lives and the clever nickname they have for their spouse, are a blight upon the media that should be stamped out. If I wanted to hear about some middle-class bint's child eating crayons and learning about life, I'd go back to lurking at Thirroul Neighbourhood Centre.

THE FUN-LOVING, FASHION-WEARING, MAN-TROUBLED, "YOU THINK YOU HAVE WEIGHT ISSUES – LISTEN TO MY LATEST STORY ABOUT TRYING TO CRAM INTO A PAIR OF 'SKINNY JEANS' BUT IN THE END WE ALL LOVE OURSELVES AND WOULD NEVER WANT TO BE KATE MOSS, ISN'T THAT RIGHT GIRLS?" COLUMNIST: Fuck Ralph Lauren, fuck *Desperate Housewives* and fuck you.

MAINSTREAM "HUMOUR" GUY: Tired jokes, hyperbole

and bad writing disguised as outrageous opinion, these columnists generally fall into one of two camps. The first tells wild and woolly yarns of his or her youth then, as the well runs dry, tries instead to find inspiration from their current lifestyle. Which, since they're a comfortable soft journo, isn't likely to be all that interesting. Of course, they can always write about their new kitten or how the wife doesn't get it. The other type's a wannabe reviewer, but prefers to take the lazy way out and mock everything they encounter. Not in a clever way, either.

There's only one problem with your work, Illawarra Mercury's Paul McInerny. It's not funny.

REVIEWERS (ALL OF 'EM): Writers who get up in the morning, crack their knuckles as they fire up the old computer, then commence a profitable day of whinging about a bunch of free shit they've been given. Like child-kings, the longer they've been at it, the worse they become.

'Jonestown', Jones out now

Chris Masters' controversial book *Jonestown* has outed the broadcaster Alan Jones as a homosexual. Many have argued that the writer should not have exposed Jones' private life, but Masters defends his decision. "It is crucial to understanding the motivations of Jones," said Masters. "And even more crucial to shifting books off the shelves."

The book discusses Jones' time as a teacher, claiming that he would watch young boys in the shower and rub their injuries. But Jones' supporters have argued that this was simply part of the standard private school curriculum.

Prime Minister John Howard, a close friend of Jones', said he didn't believe a person's sexuality was of any relevance unless Bill Heffernan wanted to expose it. "But for the record, I would be happy for Jones to be in a fulfilling homosexual relationship if it meant he wrote me fewer letters," he added.

It is too early to say whether Jones' conservative audience will stand by him, but one elderly listener has announced she intended to remain loyal. "I was worried about this because I'm a Christian," said Doris Kelly, 74, of Bella Vista. "But I asked my priest, and he said that you shouldn't hate someone just because their position made it impossible for them to admit their homosexuality."

Many who have read the book cannot understand what the fuss is about. "I'm surprised Jones is angry about his homosexuality being exposed. I thought it was his only endearing feature," one commentator said. "Without that, he would just be a greedy, power-hungry weirdo staring at kids in the shower."

Strong sales of the book in its first week have already shown that the ABC's decision not to print the book cannot be commercially justified. Managing Director Mark Scott admitted that the real reason the ABC pulled out

Jones dressed for a social outing

was because of their new anti-bias rules.

"If we had printed *Jonestown*, we would have had to have print a book that was equally complimentary of Jones," said Scott. "And our researchers just couldn't find anything worth more than a one page flyer."

Home-school shooting claims one

Real estate agent prefers missionary position, position, position

Uranium atom suffers half-life crisis

Bad novel reworked into failed screenplay

Prince William dumps Kate: cites 'poor inbreeding'

Prince William has dumped his middle-class girlfriend Kate Middleton, saying she won't make a suitable royal wife. "Kate was lovely, but ultimately we are from different social circles," William said. "If I'm going to settle down, I need to find a suitable mother for my children. And, at the same time, a long-lost cousin."

The heir-in-waiting to the British Crown is confident he will be able to find a suitable mate in his social circle before too long. "There are plenty more fish in my gene pool," he said.

Many royal-watchers have blamed the breakup on the snobbery of William's social circle. "Well-bred Englishmen would never dream of marrying so low – Kate's mother was an airline hostess, don't you know," one friend said. "They'd just give them a quickie in the aeroplane toilets and ruin their careers forever, like Ralph Fiennes did."

Other commentators point out that William may simply be planning to play the field before one day returning to his true love. "Once Wills has sowed his wild oats with the likes of Britney Spears, a few *Big Brother* contestants and half the cast of *EastEnders*, his family and friends will come to realise that Kate wasn't so déclassé after all," one said.

William's ex-girlfriend may not be lonely for long. Prince Harry, whose attitude to royal protocol is relaxed to the point of "shagging anything with a pulse", according to palace insiders, has already invited her to have a threesome with him and girlfriend Chelsy Davy.

For her part, the woman once tipped to be the future Queen is philosophical about the breakup. "If the royal family really were embarrassed by me, this could have been far worse," she said. "They could have gotten rid of me the way they got rid of Princess Diana."

Kate promised to be the most common member of the Royal Family since Fergie

Ancient Egyptians implicated in pyramid scheme

Alan Jones supports needle exchange pogrom

Novelty of novelty mug wearing off

The Chaser

Warne congratulates the only person in the world with worse hair than him.

Warne's contract with Nicorette expires.

Warne submits the first ever thesis via SMS.

WARNEY

"Farewell to the nightwatchman"

Available now from Channel Nine

Warne encounters a bigger cock than himself.

Lack of suitable dining options on the Indian tour drove Warne to breastfeed.

Warne's brief flirtation with Islam ended three hours into the Ramadan fasting.

Warne briefly considers converting to Scientology.

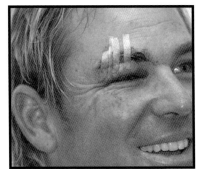

Warne's first reconciliation attempt with wife Simone.

Warne exhausts England's supply of strumpets.

Warne's most frequent Test match victim.

May 6, 1998 – the last day Warne could be lifted off the ground without mechanical aid.

Warne responds to the crowd chant, "Who ate all the pies?"

Warne edges out Mark Waugh to win the coveted Indian Bookmakers' Player Of The Year Award 1997.

Warne discovers diuretics have a laxative effect.

'Nutbush City Limits' revives party

A suburban engagement party was rescued at the eleventh hour this week, thanks to the quick thinking of a plucky DJ. Despite the open bar and extensive buffet, attendees refused to mingle, drink too much or properly celebrate the upcoming union of the guests of honour. The crisis was only averted by the narrowest of margins after the DJ finally succeeded in breaking the ice with Tina Turner's 1973 hit "Nutbush City Limits".

"It was terrible," said hostess Diana Powers. "When Macca said he and Jase were going to the pub, I nearly started crying. I spent way too much on the Chinese lantern decorations for my party to end at 10:30."

Diana's fiancé, Pete Swanston, feared the worst. "I knew the party was in trouble from the outset. For starters, no one brought their own spirits, despite us writing it in bold on the invitations. Then, Diana got pissed off because Hughsey got us the new *Wild FM* album as a gift, instead of the Corningware set she wanted."

Things looked even more dire when regular party animals Steve and Trent Businovski announced they weren't drinking because they'd been out the night before and had to work the next day. "I was counting on Steve to get things moving," said Diana. "How could he do this to me?"

When not even "The Bird Dance" coaxed guests onto the dancefloor, DJ Jordan Watts pulled out the big guns. "As

Watts carefully weighing up which Bananarama hit will really get the party jumping

soon as they heard the words, 'Church house, gin house', everyone just lined up in a grid and got ready to dance. I followed 'Nutbush' with 'Bust A Move' and then the 'Grease Megamix', and I knew things were going to be OK."

There was a brief moment of panic a few songs later, when Watts accidentally played "It's Raining Men" instead of "Love Shack". Fortunately, he was able to draw crowds back to the dancefloor by segueing quickly into Toni Basil's "Mickey".

"I think Diana and Pete will make a lovely couple," said guest Travis Hughes. "As long as they pick something catchy for the bridal waltz, like 'Shake Your Tail Feather' or 'Footloose', the wedding should go off without a hitch."

Father introduces son to lifelong hatred of fishing

Father and son in a setting of idyllic torture

Jacob Rosicky's well-meaning father has imparted to him an intense dislike for all forms of recreational angling, as well as a general antipathy for what Jacob calls "the not-so-great outdoors". Now 31, the chartered accountant need only think of fishing to bring back clear memories of freezing, pre-dawn mornings spent fiddling with a tangle.

"It must be almost twenty years ago now – but I can see my dad casting against the pre-dawn light like it was yesterday," says Rosicky, his reminiscence flowing freely. "Even then I remember thinking, 'It's 5am – what the fuck are we doing here? I wish I was in bed.'"

The inner-city resident can clearly recall images of whole, seemingly endless, days spent on the fish-free waters of a lake, the silence broken only by a bickering argument.

"It's a bit unfair to say that I hate fishing, because to be honest we spent so little time with a line in the water I'm not sure how I feel about it. I just know that someone explaining to me in remedial terms how to

thread a prawn onto a hook isn't my idea of a fun five hours. Especially on the weekend."

It was only years later, long after he'd first refused to go on a planned outing, that Rosicky recognsed the emotionally complex role that fishing trips played in his father's life. "I always knew that in a way it was an excuse for him to spend time with me, and to get half-drunk," he said. "But after we'd stopped going together, I realised his knot-tying lessons weren't about lines and lures at all, but about something much more than that. They were about patronising me," he said. "And reaching a special place where his thwarted middle-management ambitions could be played out in a pathetic power trip over his own son. For the first time I felt I really knew him as a man. A small, petty man."

Rosicky is sure he won't make the same mistake with his own son. "I'm going to let my boy find his own interests. And he's crazy about car shows, just like his old man. Isn't that right, son?"

FBI agent, pedophile find unlikely love online

Martinez during a hot date with Bute

When Special Agent Olivia Martinez started a sting operation to catch online sex predator Karl Bute Jnr, she thought it would be a routine assignment. She never suspected that the man she was entrapping would end up entrapping her heart.

The relationship had an inauspicious beginning. "My first impression was that he was a repellent, dangerous child sex offender who had shown no remorse for his crimes," said Martinez. "So I was surprised to find myself looking forward to our little chats.

"I was getting really tired of traditional dating, and kept going out with selfish egomaniacs. So to have someone be really interested in me for a change – what my hopes for the future were, what kind of clothes I liked, the route I took home from school – was really refreshing," she says.

The rapport they had developed in cyberspace didn't diminish when it came time to bring Bute into custody. "I wasn't expecting someone so, well, adorable," she said. "He looked so vulnerable being led away in handcuffs. He even brought some flowers, which was a sweet touch. So many of these pervs bring nothing more than a roll of duct-tape."

Bute, a petty criminal with a string of convictions for theft and indecent assault, was wary at first. "I generally don't like police," he says. But the two developed a natural rapport in the interview room that went beyond run-of-the-mill interrogation.

"It's the little things, you know? Asking if I need a cigarette or a cup of coffee while I'm waiting for my attorney. Being the good cop in 'good cop, bad cop'. Although she can definitely be 'bad cop' too," says Bute with a wry chuckle.

"She's a cop, and I'm a perp, so there's definitely an element of 'opposites attract'," says the former Little League coach. "But we also have common interests, like surveillance operations. I don't really think of her as being 'Special Agent' – she'll always be Strawberry_13 to me."

Martinez says she's "not 100% happy" with what she calls Bute's "lifestyle choices", but says she's trying to take things one day at a time. "Everyone has some little things about their partner they'd like to change."

While Bute's ongoing trials may throw a spanner in the works, the couple say that they can see a bright future together. "Karl says he can see kids down the track," says Martinez.

"But only with binoculars," Bute adds.

Eddie does better vs 100 than vs Seven

McGuire – may bone himself

Channel Nine CEO Eddie McGuire has returned to the small screen, hosting a gameshow that features a triumph against the odds – beating Seven in the ratings. The much-hyped show, *1 vs 100*, spent months in pre-production, as producers struggled to find 100 Nine viewers to serve as competitors.

"We had a few awkward moments, like when I asked all the contestants why they'd switched to Seven news," McGuire said. "But no one's more experienced with rabid, adversarial mobs than someone who's been the president of Collingwood. And those skills will come in handy again when I next face the PBL board."

PBL boss James Packer has denied that he is demoting McGuire. "I've told Eddie not to worry so much about the minor issues like making decisions and running the company, and to focus on the core element of the CEO's role – hosting a top-rating quiz show," he said.

"But don't worry – when it comes time to sack someone to appease shareholders, then I can guarantee Eddie will feature very prominently."

Despite the enormous pressure he faces, McGuire remains optimistic. "Nine's a tough environment, and I know that everyone here gets sacked eventually," he said. "And then goes off to Seven and has more success than ever before."

Germaine Greer struggling for insensitive angle on Brock's death

Iconoclastic feminist Germaine Greer has struggled to arrive at a contrarian position on the death of Peter Brock, having prematurely exhausted her anti-ocker arguments on Steve Irwin. It took Greer several attempts to create a tenuous link between Brock's death and a social issue of some import.

"Motor 'sport' is of course not a sport at all, and Peter Brock was not a sportsman," wrote the permanently disgruntled feminist icon, in a draft version of an opinion piece for the UK's *Guardian* newspaper. "He was a rubber-and-fuel burning environmental vandal. That one of the trees he had done so much to harm in the end came to harm him, is perhaps not surprising."

Unhappy with having to repeat the "ironic death" motif for both figures, and regretting using up her self-description as "a citizen of the rain forest" too soon, Greer then rewrote the tart piece, instead attacking Brock for his hypocritical stance on road safety. She also took the opportunity to criticise the media's anodyne and cynical commercialisation of grieving, while at the same time drawing attention to her own deep respect for Aboriginal spirituality.

"Peter Brock could not fool even himself with his belated reinvention as a road safety campaigner," she wrote, trying to muster up some indignation. "Many foolish young men who watched him emulated him off the race-track with consequences that were fatal,

Given the amount of rage she causes, Greer too may die doing what she loves best

not just to themselves, but also to the blameless drivers who got in their way."

"That Brock himself came to grief speeding on a country road is not fair, but it is fitting," wrote Greer in her conclusion. She will now attempt to make the sentiment marginally less

contrived by asserting that "many Australians will agree with me," in subsequent media interviews.

Greer is now hoping that Shane Warne will die suddenly, as she has already prepared a highly controversial post-mortem.

Meakin to spend weekend detention recruiting 'TT' guests

Oldfield denies putting 1 in Hanson's box

Warney claims adultery not the same without Simone

Howard offers to bring Hicks home on Garuda flight

Hidden Knowledge

(Not in any way affiliated with 'The Secret')

Are you feeling alone in a cold, unloving existence that seems to have no rhyme, reason or fairness? Do you want more stuff? Are you very ugly?

Fret no more! By purchasing this book, you have opened yourself to the mysterious and mystical world of HIDDEN KNOWLEDGE. No longer will you stand in supermarket checkout lines, wondering why everyone else's trolley is so much more full than yours. No more will you sit naked in your loungeroom, crying over spilled milk, chopped onions and the flies in your ointment.

All you have to do is follow the sacred and ineffable laws of HIDDEN KNOWLEDGE, and the universe will open its cosmic arms to you with love and respect, just as it did to other HIDDEN KNOWLEDGE followers like Le Comte de St-Germain, Julius Caesar and Emilio Estevez.

How does it work?

The pseudoscientific principles behind HIDDEN KNOWLEDGE are a galactic enigma guarded by naked, bearded feng shui experts from the East and lab coat-wearing geniuses from Earth's most prestigious learning academies. In short, the astromechanics of HIDDEN KNOWLEDGE are far, far beyond your meagre faculties, but we can boil it down for you:

If something bad happens, it's probably your fault.

How can I stop bad things happening to me?

That's right. If your parents split up, your husband gets prostate cancer or your daughter is impregnated by a moustachioed hoodlum from the wrong side of the tracks, you have only yourself to blame. Instead of following the divine ruleset handed down from the Elder God, you've been unconsciously wishing for trauma and penury to blacken your soul. That's why Donald Trump is a billionaire with a beautiful young wife while all those children are starving in Uganda – the African kids don't have HIDDEN KNOWLEDGE.

Before you read on, take a deep breath and think about what you really, really want out of life. Close your eyes and picture the things that would make you feel happy and content. Now, forget those goals. They're the pathetic dreams of a total loser and frankly, they're embarrassing. HIDDEN KNOWLEDGE will replace those mundane aims with the aspirations of a sultan, a dictator... or even a demigod!

Step One: ASK
That's it. Ask. All you have to do to get started on the road to success is ask. Ask passersby for change. Ask your new girlfriend for her PIN number. Ask attractive bar patrons for sex. Ask your enemies to kneel before you. It doesn't matter what you ask for. The important thing is to demand something from others. Something you don't have, but want.

Step Two: IMAGINE
Did you know that humans have the ability to imagine things that don't exist? No other animal, except perhaps those gorillas who know sign language, has that skill. Now, you can harness that talent and make it work for you! Sit on the floor of your shanty and cross your legs. Breathe slowly, in through your nose and out through your mouth. This is the tricky part. You have to form a mental picture of the things you asked for in Step One. It's no good wanting a slice of pie If you can't conjure up a mental image of the blueberries inside, is it? Once that mind picture is firmly in place, you're ready to move onto Step Three: Communing With The Universe.

Step Four: GET
Now that you've made contact with the supreme tentacled wonder that is cosmic superconsciousness, and it has understood your darkest desires, all you need to do is sit back in that antique rocking chair your grandfather put together with his bare hands, and wait.

Remember: IF SOMETHING BAD HAPPENS, IT'S PROBABLY YOUR FAULT.

Congratulations. You have the key, and you have HIDDEN KNOWLEDGE.

Printer's note

Step Three: Communing With The Universe was accidentally left out of the above article. You can gain a copy of the missing text by sending a stamped, self-addressed envelope and a money order for $499.95 to Hidden Knowledge, c/o The Chaser.

Hilali given the sack: forces his wife to wear it

Sheikh Taj El-Din Hilali has agreed not to give any more sermons at the Lakemba mosque, following the intervention of fellow Muslims, or as the sheikh called them, "Islamaphobes".

The controversial cleric was also forced to deny that he was a bigot who hated Australia. "I think Australia is the greatest Satanic infidel country full of lying convicts in the world. I didn't wish to offend anyone, except idolaters and Jews," he said, in a statement that was immediately taken out of context.

Hilali first found himself in hot water with his comments that Freemasons ran the world and that women were to blame for rape, which were condemned in all quarters except the Gibson household.

Sent overseas to lie low, Hilali then appeared on an Egyptian breakfast television show, where he claimed that Westerners were the "world's greatest liars", forcing the bemused host to finish the planned electro-magnetic mattress advertorial by himself.

"The diatribe could have been a mistake," admitted one advisor. "Then again, you have to admit the host asked for it, the way he dressed."

Hilali's fledging political career also seems to have stalled, with Hilali denying he has made a deal with NSW Opposition Leader Peter Debnam. "I wouldn't go near Debnam," he said "Some of his colleagues in the NSW Libs are real nutjobs."

However, the NSW Opposition remain wary. "Hilali said voters were infidels and the biggest liars in the world," said one insider. "But Peter still can't seem to beat him in the polls."

Hilali claims he saved this baby from a Jew's pie

It's understood the Sheikh will now retire from the public eye and limit his commentary to less heated issues such as abortion, euthanasia and Northern Ireland.

Precocious 2nd grader writes memoir of holidays

Set the topic, "What I did during my holidays" as a class writing assignment, eight-year-old student Bradley K. Milton has produced a discursive Proustian reminiscence, heavy with nostalgia for a youth that somehow seems weeks ago. The foolscap page-long *roman à clef*, written in pencil, is a vision of a happier, simpler time in the author's life, when days were measured only by the opening and closing hours of Warner Brothers' Movie World.

"Those days come back to me as one," the young dilettante wrote, after a brief introductory exegesis on the subject of memory. "One endless day, suffused with laughter and golden light, taking place in no place but in my pure state of happiness, extant now only in my mind, and perhaps not even there, for even those eyes through which I saw my childhood have now grown cloudy with age, and some solid thing, perhaps time itself, begins to occlude my memory, waking me from my reveries as clearly as the sound of the bell for recess."

His stream-of-consciousness in free flow, Bradley then attempted a subtle, symbolic conflation of the long car trip to the Gold Coast and the complex emotional undercurrents in his seemingly happy family.

"The time-share apartment was not the domain of my mother, who acquiesced to the role of a subordinate with a kind of relieved resignation, a sentiment, that in time, my sister and I came to share: for it was Aunt Anne who fussed over us – cooking, cleaning, keeping a happy vigil from the sand as we paddled in the foam – she played with us, though shyly, (and with that spirit of interminable enthusiasm peculiar to the childless), and it was she who felt the end of those sunlit days most keenly,

her drawn face coloured a muted azure by the tinting on the Subaru's back window and the light of the setting sun, the waves of her hand ebbing into a blur in the distance as we drove quickly away – I see it ever clear even now, some eleven days later."

Bradley's next work is expected to be on the topic "The person I admire most", and he plans to write it about himself.

Unlike Proust, Bradley is unfortunately not confined to his bedroom

The Chaser

Rudd offers voters a 'dork in the road'

For once, Rudd isn't the only one who's pleased with himself

Buoyed by strong early results in opinion polls, Kevin Rudd is offering voters an unprecedented choice between two nerds in the 2007 election.

"The public can rest assured that no matter who wins the election, they will be led by an uncharismatic, socially conservative man with glasses and a bad haircut," the new Leader of the Opposition said.

Rudd says Australia must now choose what kind of country it wants to be. "I am offering voters a clear choice," he said, "between the legacy of German pastor and political theorist Dietrich Bonhoeffer and the doctrinaire Austrian-school neo-liberalism of Friedrich von Hayek," said Rudd. "I guess what I'm really asking is *quis custodes ipsos custodient?*"

The epigram has already been backed by Labor *eminence grise* Gough Whitlam as an election slogan.

Rudd then repeated his comments in Mandarin Chinese to emphasise his major point of difference with John Howard. "I am going to to to show the electorate that I can sound smug not only in English and Mandarin, but also Vietnamese, Tagalog, Lao, and several of those clicking languages spoken by hill tribes," Rudd said.

"That'll show John Howard. Or as they say in Myanmar, *"chi lai bu dan* John Howard."

But Rudd's strong poll figures have made Labor insiders fear a rerun of Mark Latham's crippling 2004 defeat. John Howard is struggling against him in Parliament, sending waves of panic around the ALP party room. "We've seen this before, a new face with fresh ideas who attracts voters in droves – until election day when they switch back to Howard," one long-time MP said. "We should have stuck with Kim Beazley. At least he didn't get our hopes up."

Other Labor figures have been reassuring themselves that Rudd could never become another Latham. "That combination of a faulty pancreas and hyperactive bile duct was unique," one backbencher said. "And Kevin Rudd would never break a cabbie's arm. He'd be too busy trying out his Chinese on them."

But most old hands remain pessimistic. "When the latest new hope fails at the next election, we'll find ourselves having to turn back to experience once more," one minister said. "And I don't know that the party can survive being led by Simon Crean again."

Boyfriend dumped after unfavourable 'Cleo' quiz result

A relationship quiz entitled Is He The One? that appeared in a recent issue of *Cleo* has led Sydney woman Jane Kurkova to break off her engagement with truck driver Miles Daly. Kurkova was "shocked and heartbroken" when her fiancé scored a mere four out of twenty, putting him firmly in the "Dump this frickin' loser already" category.

"I was devastated," she said. "I thought we were happy. But *Cleo* reckons his long-haul road trips, delivering goods across the country, are neglectful and a sign he could be having an affair. So I knew what I had to do."

Further inspection of Kurkova's completed quiz showed Miles's poor performance in several categories, including listening skills, flower-purchasing and preferred magazines. "I had no idea Jane was monitoring my reading preferences," he said. "If I'd known *MAD*, *Viz* and *People* were gonna end my relationship, I might've picked up *The Bulletin* now and again."

Kurkova informed Miles of his poor results when he returned home after a 14-hour stint at work. "He looked so stunned when I told him I wanted to back out of the whole thing, but Miles had no argument when I showed him the quiz results. And he refused to wash up after dinner – just as question 7 predicted."

Taking a break from approving a feature on how to attract a new man the Britney Spears way, *Cleo* editor Nedahl Stelio said: "Our quizzes are just a bit of fun – like the rest of our magazine, you're not supposed to take them too seriously. Maybe we need a Cleo Quiz Gullibility Test?"

Stelio later admitted, however, that she hires all new writers for her magazine on the basis of the *Cleo* Soul Mate Test.

Kurkova conducting scientific research

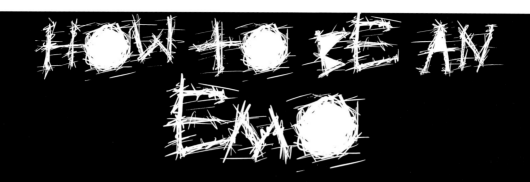

RULE ONE

If anyone calls you emo, deny it until your dying breath.

Now that key instruction is out of the way, we can get down to brass tacks.

MUSIC

This is a tricky one, because you don't want to be pinned down to anything specific (see Rule #1). All we can tell you is that you must be prepared to disavow enjoyment or knowledge of any band as soon as they become known to everyone else who claims they aren't emo.

ATTITUDE

Give off the impression that you think the world's against you. Since you're a spoilt, whiny, overprivileged teenager, it pretty much is. Ideally, your friends will feel like they are the last barrier between you and sucide – which means they'll put up with a great deal of self-indulgent shit from you.

POETRY

Your poetry should be full of dark imagery, and reflect the pain and anguish of your soul. If you can't think of anything to write about, just lie back on your bed, think about all the bullshit things your parents, teachers, so-called friends and that girl you like have done to you this week, then let the mascara-stained tears (and lyrics about being trapped in a heartless web of lies not of your making) flow.

APPEARANCE

Hair: Black, obviously, with a side fringe that just covers one eye. This will give the impression that you're too weary with the horrors of the world to brush your hair behind your ear.

EYES

Black eyeliner will really bring out the haunted sensitivity of your dark, soulful eyes, letting everyone know that you have suffered, truly suffered.

MOUTH

Lipstick is optional, but the main thing is to remember not to smile. At most, you're allowed to sneer with superior malice.

SHIRT

You can go with a band shirt, but if someone takes a photo of you endorsing The Used, it's going to be hard to pretend you always hated them later (a common tactic is to claim you wore the shirt ironically).

COAT

Make sure the sleeves on your vaguely militaristic-looking coat are just long enough to almost cover your self-injury scars. You don't want to look like you're showing them off, but remember – you can't get sympathy if no one sees the physical signs of your tortured, artistic pain.

PANTS

I dunno. Just like, whatever's lying around. NB: Make sure "whatever's lying around" is a carefully selected pair of trousers that accurately convey the impression that you're a hard-done-by victim who doesn't even need to try to look fashionable.

SHOES

Either scuffed boots or battered black sneakers. A wounded bird like you can't be bothered lifting their feet to take proper steps.

THINGS TO SAY

- "I've never liked My Chemical Romance. They suck."
- "I think I'm gonna go home. Alone. Again. Sigh."
- "You just don't understand what I need."
- "Even artists don't understand my work – that's why they criticise it."
- "I can't believe you'd go out of your way to hurt my feelings like this."
- "You're such an emo."

English teacher writes novel about teaching English

Although her weekdays are spent educating Wollongong students on the importance of Shakespeare, Emily Dickinson and Peter Goldsworthy, English teacher Sharne Mitchell, 48, has a deeper passion – her magnum opus on the turbulent inner life of a late-40s woman who educates Wollongong students on the importance of Shakespeare, Emily Dickinson and Peter Goldsworthy.

Mitchell's *Dusty Textbooks & Liquid Paper* is, in her own words, "a dark and gritty exploration of love, learning and the trials of being Supervisor Of Girls." At 450 pages, the novel spans four terms in the life of Relieving Deputy Head Teacher – English, Rae Sjostedt.

"I used Conrad's *Heart Of Darkness* as a kind of framework and inspiration for *Dusty Textbooks*," Mitchell said. "In the same way Marlow traverses the waters of the Congo River to find a spiritual barbarism within himself, Rae braves the murky depths of bottom Year 10 poetry to find they have no knowledge of rhyme, metaphor or iambic pentameter."

Mitchell has also worked in some of her experiences as a Rock Eisteddfod co-ordinator: "Nothing can compare to the dizzying highs and crashing lows that accompany a hundred teenage girls in leotards, dancing in unison to U2's 'With Or Without You'. I've used the 'Fod experience to mirror Rae's fruitless search for a staffroom soulmate."

Some critics have chided Mitchell for basing certain characters on real-life people, but the author claims she was careful to avoid direct analogues. "People think Neil 'Butch' Wilde is based on [Year 8 bully] Beau Wiles, but he's more of an amalgam of all the fat, obnoxious loudmouths I've had in my classroom over my 21 years of teaching."

Dusty Textbooks & Liquid Paper is yet to be picked up by a publisher, but Mitchell remains confident it will eventually be included on the HSC syllabus. She has also commenced work on a sequel, tentatively titled *Beyond The Chalkface*. "It's more of a fantasy work," she explained. "Following the painful demise of Neil Wilde, Rae wins the lottery and is able to retire to southern France, where she drinks champagne, writes moving sonnets and has a whirlwind romance with a young, handsome gardener."

Sharne in what she hopes will be her author photo

7-Eleven clerk lives vicariously through condom purchaser

Russell gazes into the middle distance, wondering who Steve's having sex with right now

Convenience store duty manager Russell Celine spends most of his 6pm-4am shifts serving truck drivers, drunk uni students and late-night porn buyers, but there is one highlight in his ten hours of drudgery – imagining what kind of sexual debauchery regular condom buyer Steve Tintoski gets up to. Although Celine has never actually seen Tintoski accompanied by a woman, he often fantasises about the "raw, animal carnality that guy must have inside him".

"Steve comes in here two, three times a week," said Celine, who hasn't required a condom since his girlfriend dumped him six months ago. "He always buys a 12-pack of Ansell Lifestyles condoms and a two-litre bottle of Coke Zero. I just can't imagine anyone being able to burn through so many rubbers in such a short period of time. He must have, like, five girlfriends. Or maybe just one hot nympho who can't get enough."

Compounding the unintentionally celibate clerk's jealous admiration is the fact Tintoski always purchases large-sized condoms and is constantly taking phone calls on his mobile. "So not only is he getting more action than Shane Warne on tour – he's well-endowed, too. What a legend. I bet he's slept with all sorts of babes. Probably some famous chicks as well. I wonder if he knows Krystal from *Big Brother*."

Although the two have barely spoken beyond the usual transaction and customer service niceties, Celine feels a kinship with his favourite customer. "When I tell Steve to 'Have a good night', he knows what I'm talking about. One time, he bought a packet of black condoms. That time, I said, 'Have a great night!'"

Celine plans to ask the condom purchaser what he's doing Friday night, in the hopes of gaining more insight into Tintoski's sex life. "Who knows? Maybe he can give me a few pointers for picking up that blonde who always buys *NW* and a pack of peppermint Extra."

MMM – CHEMICAL FLAVOURS WITH A HINT OF AMMONIA... INTENSE TO EXCRUCIATING PAIN...

WINE CRITIC SUICIDE.

Rudd achieves nuclear disarmament of Garrett

Rudd and Garrett use interpretative dance to explain their new nuclear proliferation policy

In what may be his biggest victory yet, Opposition Leader Kevin Rudd has unilaterally disarmed formerly outspoken anti-nuclear activist Peter Garrett. The Shadow Minister for Climate Change, Environment, Heritage and the Arts had his anti-uranium core removed and deactivated by the new leader in a delicate operation that took place hours before the 2007 Labor national conference.

By disarming Garrett, Rudd has neatly avoided the threat of mutually assured destruction, a theoretical scenario in which economically unpopular policies lead the business community to uniformly endorse the re-election of John Howard. This, analysts say, would trigger a harsh, three-year nuclear winter that Labor would struggle to survive.

"I'm very proud to announce that Mr Garrett is now 100% safe and opinion-free," said Rudd, in an address to the party faithful. "He poses absolutely no threat to the health and wellbeing of Australia's aspirational voters, business lobbyists or mining executives. Rest assured, when Peter sings 'If I work all day in the Blue Sky Mine, there'll be food on the table tonight', he's no longer being ironic."

Garrett was quick to dismiss accusations

he has become a puppet of ALP heavies. "As a team player, I've merely adopted Kevin's slogan of 'Fresh thinking'," he explained. "By making an abrupt about-face on topics like the US-Australia alliance and Pine Gap, I've been able to bring other environmental issues to the forefront of this electoral campaign. For example, both sides of politics are now paying valuable lip service to the issue of climate change."

With Rudd having successfully rendered all members of his Cabinet inert as he prepares to fight the next election, experts say that the most likely Australian politician to produce an uncontrollable meltdown is now Bill Heffernan.

Rudd expels union hacks: front bench decimated

Howard finally names greenhouse target: Peter Garrett

Keating blames outbursts on 'the depression I had to have'

Woolmer not murdered at World Cup, unlike Pakistan

14-year-old anarchist uses Sex Pistols logo as MSN Messenger picture

In an effort to inform friends and family of his new-found political awareness, Joss Freeman, 14, has changed his MSN Messenger display picture from a photo of his cat to a stylised Sex Pistols logo.

"I'm an anarchist," he said in a brief break between rounds of his favourite first-person shooter, Counterstrike. "I've been reading about Billy Bragg and Joe Strummer on Wikipedia, and I reckon we should smash the state. Thatcher has to go."

Since discovering the revolutionary music of late 1970s England, the Wollongong native has completely changed the way he feels about a range of issues from the role of the monarchy in Britain to the appropriateness of spitting in public.

"After watching *The Filth and the Fury*, I started a blog called 'Never Mind The Bollocks, Here's Joss'. I write a lot about class warfare, The Clash and Gizbie, my character in World Of Warcraft."

Other anarchy-embracing measures Joss has taken include asking for a guitar for his birthday, putting safety pins through his schoolbag and only developing crushes on girls with dyed hair and nose rings.

"I'm not too worried about it," says Joss's mum Sonya, who supplied the credit card the young anarchist used to order a "God Save The Queen" T-shirt online. "His older brother used to be right into

Freeman proudly wears an anarchic haircut

Jim Morrison, Donovan and rejecting the corporate world, and he's been working for Westpac since he finished Year 12."

HOW TO START YOUR OWN LADS MAG

So, you've seen how those lad mag blokes live and you want in. Workdays spent lazing around the office, tossing footballs, ogling bikini babes and waiting for free tickets to sporting events. Invitations to celebrity poker tournaments and crocodile wrestling. Sounds pretty sweet, doesn't it? And all you have to do in return is bash out a few thousand words a week.

Of course, before you get to that point, you're gonna have to actually set up your magazine and sell it to the public. This article will help you avoid a few of the pitfalls that have befallen lesser would-be lads.

TITLE

Naming your magazine is the most important step in the whole process, so we'll get it out of the way early. What you're looking for is a single word that captures exactly what you're about – something to sum up the special blend of rough-around-the-edges blokiness, faux blue-collar sensibilities and unbridled exuberance for all things female. You might also want to consider capitalising the whole name. Here's a few sample titles:

Brick, sloth, BALLS, RooT, ABATTOIR

MASCOT

Next, you need two mascots. The first should be a furry animal like a weasel or dingo. The second should be an ex-Big Brother contestant with massive tits and a large collection of skimpy underwear. Both your mascots should appear on as many covers as possible, as well as pop up throughout the mag to comment on articles through the medium of witty puns in speech bubbles.

COLUMNISTS

Obviously you don't want to waste your time writing articles when you could be schmoozing with models and reviewing beers at the local, so you'll want to hire a crack team of columnists to do the heavy lifting for you. Fortunately, there are plenty of pencil-squeezers out there stinging to work for a magazine like yours.

◊ **A hot woman (see image above)** – To save on costs, you can get your mascot (the babe, not the furry animal) to do this job. The hot woman's perfect for running your mag's sex column, dispensing advice on picking up chicks, broaching the subject of a threesome with one's girlfriend's sister and whether or not ladies should swallow. It's a proven fact that readers prefer a sex columnist with huge bosoms over a squirrely bloke with glasses. And if your mascot can't write for shit, just get the squirrely bloke to ghost-write her advice. As long as he avoids mentioning his penis in the text, no one will know the difference.

◊ **A blokey bloke** – If he looks like a hardened criminal, so much the better. He can run your letters column, where he can most effectively question the

sexuality of correspondents and hand out prizes to those he deems most "hard". If you need to fill another page, the blokey bloke can also write opinion pieces on the death of the

Aussie battler, how homosexual Australia has become, and whatever happened to the ANZAC spirit. And if he can't write for shit, that's OK. He's a symbol of our national pride in being uneducated.

◊ **A squirrely techno-geek bloke** – This guy serves two purposes. One, he lets your readers know what's happening in the world of games and technological gadgets, keeping them informed and the sponsors happy. Two, he lets your readers feel superior to the squirrely bloke who spends all his time setting up binary alarm clocks and playing

Twilight Princess on the Wii. And if the squirrely bloke can't write for shit, just get your mascot to ghost-write his reviews. As long as she avoids mentioning sex in the text, no one will know the difference.

◊ **A celebrity** – It's a little-known fact that most of the "funny" people you see on TV can't write for shit, so while it adds value to have their photo at the top of a

weekly column about everything and nothing (which means they'll drone on about their kids, pets, sex and the differences between men and women), the actual written content will need shitloads of retooling. Celebrities are precious, too, so make sure you never, ever take a phone call from them, demanding to know why their golden prose was altered by a ghost-writing team consisting of your mascot and techno-geek.

OTHER CONTENT

Once your columnists are wrangled, you'll need stuff to fill out the other 82 or so pages of your glossy publication. Hopefully a significant amount of space will be taken up with ads for mobile phone wallpapers about the guy from Scream smoking marijuana and jokes implying the owner has been fucking other people's

mothers, but the rest of the magazine is going to require content. Here are some time-tested, sure-fire winners:

◊ **Sex confessions from readers**

◊ **Photos of brutal injuries from readers**

◊ **"Hilarious" photos stolen from the internet and sent in by readers**

◊ **Salacious stories about American gangs or hardened criminals**

◊ **Interviews with whoever you can con into letting you interview them**

◊ **Reviews of whatever films and concerts you can con publicists into sending you to**

DESIGN BRIEF

The impression you want to give, when someone looks at your magazine, is that a bunch of knockabout fellas chucked a bunch of stuff together and threw in a few fart jokes. It is important to know that if you actually did this, no one in the world would want to read your piece of shit publication. It takes a lot of hard work to make a magazine look like a visual tribute to studied indifference. But here are a few pointers:

◊ **Cut down on words. No one's reading them anyway**

◊ **Any time you can add a caption, breakout box or pointer, you must do so**

◊ **Mix it up a little – include screen captures stolen from films and tearsheets nicked from foreign mags**

◊ **Let these five words be your mantra: bright colours and crazy fonts**

◊ **If you're going to talk about, say, the 'Sopranos' finale months before it's screened in Australia, make sure to print a small "spoiler warning" sticker right next to the giant photos that fans of the show would really want to avoid looking at**

FINAL WORD

That's it! Congratulations, you're on your way to guaranteed magazine success! As long as you can ignore the complaints and views of your feminist friends and colleagues, feel free to kick back in your expensive leather office chair, hands behind your head, and wait for the cash, babes and good times to flow.

UN Security Council fails to enforce New Year's resolution

The UN Security Council has admitted it is in clear breach of its own 2007 New Year's Resolution. SC Resolution #1738, which stated council members would "Join the gym – and this time really stick with it" was struck in a mood of optimism at the first meeting of the year. However, it waned through March and April, and has now "floundered completely", as a spokesman put it.

The council is also in breach of several prior resolutions including 1729 ("The council resolves…that we really need to get in shape"), and sanctions could now follow.

"This issue has proven more difficult to enforce than we anticipated," said an aide to the current UNSC President. "Striking a compromise between sovereignty and the will of the diplomatic community is always fraught, and it turns out that after work, we're usually pretty tired and just want to put our feet up." The aide also stated that the group's previous New Year's resolution, "That the council quit smoking", could also be a contributing factor. "It's hard to do everything at once," he said. "Baby steps, you know?"

While no one is taking the blame for the fiasco, fingers are being pointed at individual member states. The UK had acted to water down the original wording of the resolution, arguing that it should instead read "maybe we should start doing some Pilates." France is also under scrutiny for adding a sub-section suggesting delegates could still "have the occasional piece of gateau, just as a treat."

China almost derailed the process single-handedly by abstaining from the resolution altogether. "We question the wisdom of a binding resolution of this kind," said the Chinese representative. "It's not even our New Year."

Delegates say they hope to cobble together a new resolution in time to ensure the Council is looking good for summer.

The Council debating a waistline non-proliferation treaty

Girl suspects Tom from MySpace not fully committed to friendship

New MySpace user Emily Lee, 14, says she feels neglected by her new friend, the company's CEO Tom Anderson. Lee was delighted when she first signed up for the site and found she already had him listed as a friend, and had even received a message from the man she describes as a "really cool guy". But now she is beginning to doubt that Tom looked at her profile at all, "if that is even his real name".

"Tom's message was so sweet. He said that if I had any questions, comments, or just wanted to "say Hi", I should feel free to send him a message," she said. "I thought he was really friendly, so I just sent him a quick hello, and a bit of info on who I am and stuff. You'd think that being CEO, he'd be logged on the whole time. But he hasn't even replied in, like, three whole weeks.

"So I messaged him a few more times, just in case he'd accidentally deleted it," she said. "I even asked him if he'd like to go bowling or something next time he's in Australia – not as a date or anything, just to hang out, you know? And still nothing. I'm starting to feel like he sees me as just another one of the 176,507,259 he's got listed on his profile. And I'm not going to pretend it doesn't hurt a little bit.

"He signed off that initial message by saying 'I'll see you on MySpace!' I never thought I'd say this of a friend, but I'm starting to think those words were empty," she said.

Since her disappointment with Tom, though, Emily's MySpace social life has started to look up. "After a few weeks, I've discovered that there are lots of people who want to be my friend," she said. "Although nearly all of them are indie bands whose

Emily disputes Tom's claim that MySpace is "a place for friends"

music sounds a bit crap. Still, you've got to feel flattered."

Fortunately, Emily has now received messages from several older gentlemen who have expressed an interest in meeting up in person, especially if she wears the school uniform from her profile photo.

Zimbabwean cricket team backs calls for Australian boycott

The Australian Government's call for Ricky Ponting's side to abandon its tour to Zimbabwe has been echoed by their opponents. "We've suffered enough in this country without having to get thrashed by Australia again," captain Prosper Utseya said.

"In my view, being made to face Brett Lee when you've only made the team because

of a racially biased selection policy is cruel and unusual punishment," he said.

But the Zimbabwe Cricket Union insists that the home team has a chance, pointing out that due to the rapid inflation crisis currently affecting the country, the Australian XI would be facing off against the Zimbabwean MCCCXXIV.

In a fiery speech, Mugabe slammed John Howard for being racist, offering to forcibly displace the Prime Minister from Kirribilli House and hand it back to the black population. Mugabe's position has won him support from Bob Brown and Margo Kingston.

In a bid to resolve the deadlock, the ICC has suggested the game be played at a neutral venue, but the Zimbabwean Government angrily disagreed. "We are tired of this

sort of interference from the international community, who do not understand how Zimbabwe works," President Mugabe said. "Next they'll be suggesting that we hold our elections at neutral venues."

Prime Minister John Howard says that if the tour is allowed to proceed, the oppressive Zimbabwean regime will be handed a publicity coup, an allegation that Mugabe quickly dismissed. "It's ridiculous to say that I am seeking propaganda benefits from the tour," he said. "The country's newspapers will write positive headlines about me whether the Australians play or not."

President Mugabe has said that if the Australians don't ultimately end up touring, his security forces are equally adept at beating Zimbabweans.

Rudd to attend fake memorial at Virginia Tech

Kevin Rudd has again come under fire after plans for a fake memorial for the victims of the Virginia Tech massacre became public. "I knew nothing about a plan for a fake service for the *Sunrise* show," Rudd said this morning. "I thought it was for a *60 Minutes* colour piece."

Producers have now abandoned their plans for the earlier, staged service, which they denied was disrespectful. "It was a dignified service plan," said the *Sunrise* exec. "Our only departures from protocol were that the planned minute of silence be split into two thirty-second halves, to prevent bored viewers changing channels. And that the Dean give his eulogy inside a tent, to maintain exclusivity."

Sunrise has attempted to deflect criticism by pointing out that the planned event was carbon-neutral. But Virginia Tech authorities remain unsatisfied. "We're a little surprised that Mr Rudd would put himself forward to give a reading. And we're not sure who David Koch is, but he wasn't our first choice for MC."

Having backed away from the bogus event, Mr Rudd will instead appear on *Sunrise's* high-rating US equivalent, the NBC *Today* show. "I'm there to convey the message that Australia stands by these people in their hour of need," he said. "I've already written it on a sign, and I'll be holding it up outside the window. Let the healing begin."

The Opposition Leader says that he hopes some good will come of the massacre. "I

Solemn: Rudd was moved to tears in the second take

hope that we can learn something from this tragedy about this troubled young man, and how he was able to garner such an extraordinary amount of media attention."

Yeltsin remembered for getting on tank, getting tanked

Boris Yeltsin died this week after winning a protracted battle with communism, and losing a protracted battle with alcoholism. The former Russian President was best known for defying the coup plotters who attempted to depose Mikhail Gorbachev when he bravely climbed on top of a tank to see where the nearest bar was.

His friends and families allies gathered for a wake to commemorate the life of the former leader, which his widow described as "how Boris would have wanted to be remembered, if he'd ever been sober enough to state a preference." Blood alcohol tests showed that even though the event took place five days after his death, Mr Yeltsin was still the most intoxicated person at the event.

Yeltsin was the first ruler of Russia in centuries to leave the position voluntarily, resigning his post at the end of 1999. "He was concerned, as many of us were, that his alcoholism was compromising his leadership, and he recognised that something would have to give," his successor Vladimir Putin remembers. "As much as Boris loved being the first leader of the new democratic Russia, there were no surprises which one he gave away."

Putin announced that, as the founder of modern Russia, Mr Yeltsin's body will be permanently displayed in Red Square alongside Lenin's, which is preserved in formaldehyde. Yeltsin had been preparing for the honour for many years by pickling his body in vodka.

Yeltsin: forever red (faced)

PhD student regrets choosing 'Buffy the Vampire Slayer' as thesis topic

Almost four years into her 100,000-word PhD in Visual Communications, Janet Wasserman is beginning to sincerely regret her chosen area of inquiry. Her still-incomplete thesis, entitled *The perverse in the Buffyverse: RE:reading performative gender roles and their subversion in Buffy the Vampire Slayer*, has become something of an embarrassment to her.

"When I was finishing my Masters in Gender Studies, critical engagement with *Buffy* was all the rage," said the 29-year-old industrial music enthusiast. "But I'm going to finish just in time for it to be completely passé. All the important, exciting work now is being done on *Angel*."

Five years ago, Wasserman believed that Buffy was a "uniquely nuanced cultural text", a view she now believes was prompted solely by her enthusiasm for the popular TV show. "I thought that *Buffy* was a new type of cultural apparatus that could establish the co-ordinates of a more fluid, less repressive form of gendered indentity," she says. "But looking back, I think I just had the hots for Giles."

Studying *Buffy* for a doctoral thesis, an idea she once found politically progressive, now seems both cliched and rather childish, particularly now that the show is no longer on TV. "My central – and really only – idea was to look at how *Buffy* subverts gender norms by shifting the co-ordinates of received modes of performative gender construction. To be honest it's just stuff cribbed from Judith Butler," she admits.

"Worst of all, it's only good for about 20,000 words, and the rest is just repeating

Wasserman is also starting to critically rethink her hairstyle

the same idea with different examples. Strengthening my case, or 'padding' if you want to be more accurate."

Attending a conference on *Buffy* successfully destroyed her remaining faith in academia. "It was all goths, repressed gays and punning session titles. After Fangs for the Mammaries, how could I go on?" And her love for what was once her favourite TV show is set to be the next victim. "I was naïve enough to think that

I could never get sick of *Buffy*," she says. "Boy, was I wrong about that."

Chastened by her experience, Wasserman hopes her mistake can serve as a lesson to others. "I'd say now that if someone wants to waste their time with on an exhaustive treatment of a flash-in-the-pan pop-culture phenomenon, they shouldn't do it at University," she says. "That's what Wikipedia is for."

A history of video games

Since everyone else is too busy playing Mario Kart on the bus, trying to remember what they found arousing about Leisure Suit Larry and reminiscing about that time they scored a flawless victory against their upstart cousin in Mortal Kombat, we've taken it upon ourselves to record the complete and utter history of videogames for posterity. And to make the thing we've wasted so many hours of our lives doing seem somehow important.

The dim, dark past

Before videogames were invented, people had to amuse themselves with more primitive interaction, like throwing Frisbees at each other, swapping rooks for bishops and eating picnic lunches at the beach. It was a boring, dreary time, when mowing down hordes of ravenous hellspawn with a railgun was something you had to imagine in your head. Barbarous.

'Pong' and all that

Thankfully, nerds had grown weary of recreating WW2 battles with cardboard chits and paper maps, and were looking for the next big thing to occupy their time. There's a lot of arguments over which videogame was the first, but we're gonna bypass all that and say it was Pong. This primitive recreation of meatspace activity Ping Pong sprang fully formed from the brain of Mr Atari in 1972. In what would be the model for every videogame to follow, Pong took something physical, interactive and fun, and turned it into an addictive, repetitive preoccupation that will inevitably leave you fat and alone.

The Golden Age of Arcade Games

The next wave of machines to steal our time, money and eyesight was characterised by pretty colours and insane storylines. Sure, in Space Invaders you were protecting the planet from predictable aliens, but it's a tribute to the utter lack of entertainment options in the early 1980s that people so readily accepted a yellow disc that eats pellets while it runs away from ghosts, or a giant ape called Donkey who kidnaps women then throws endless barrels at a moustachioed guy in a red hat and overalls. Oh, and the less said about goddamn Dig Dug, the better. Tunneling through dirt to inflate goggle-wearing, monstrous tomatoes until they pop is

a completely insane way to spend your time, no matter what year it is.

Home invasion

Two types of systems invaded our homes in the wake of the Golden Age Of Arcade Games: consoles and computers. Both were designed to eliminate the need for any kind of exercise or human interaction, since now game geeks didn't even have to walk down to the arcade to get their fix of Frogger. They could stay home and help amphibians avoid traffic. Even better, the titles on home computers began expanding in complexity – instead of monotonously destroying row after row of bad guys, players could thrill to the idea of destroying row after row of bad guys in levels with different backgrounds...and sometimes even different music!

Plumbers, platforms and porcupines

A bunch more stuff happened, then a man by the name of Mr Nintendo had the brilliant idea of taking the dude from Donkey Kong and putting him in his own game about mushrooms that make you taller, teleportation pipes filled with carnivorous plants and punching bricks so hard that coins fly

Quake's monsters are almost as terrifying as the game's fans find women

out of them. Super Mario Bros was such a massive hit that Mr Nintendo's closest competitor, a moustachioed villain named Professor Sega, was forced to invent a game about a blue hedgehog who collects rings and gives children seizures to stay in the arms race.

Blockheads ascendant

With all the amazing developments in graphics, storylines and overall gameplay, the world waited in quiet expectation for the next big thing that would rock the videogaming universe to its very core with sheer breathtaking awesomeness. The winner? A bunch of coloured blocks falling in random order. Still, at least Tetris was more fun than Minesweeper – and so addictive that people would dream about rotating tetrominoes.

Shooting Nazis, demons, bullies, etc.

Nerds have engaged in revenge fantasies since time immemorial, but it wasn't until the release of first-person shooters like Wolfenstein 3D, Doom and Quake that they could really cut loose in a cathartic way. Plus, those games really honed the targeting skills for those unbalanced, trenchcoat-wearing victims who wanted to take things a step further, but couldn't afford lessons at the local shooting range. Um, I mean...that was a dark chapter in the history of videogames. A dark, dark chapter that should've been avoided. Let's move on, shall we?

Combat evolves, humans don't

Meanwhile, the home console market was still going strong. Microsoft waded into the fray, causing uncounted dorkgasms with Halo: Combat Evolved, an Xbox title that let you run over your mates with a jeep when you got sick of peppering them with crystalline needles or launching rockets into their face at close range. You could play it online as well, assuming you enjoyed being totally humiliated by smartarse 12-year-olds who would shoot you dead, hump your character's corpse then call you a fag over the headset.

PSWiib0

In the past two years, a war has raged. A battle more bloody and horrific than anything the Middle East or American government could dream up. Rabid fanboys have argued back and forth across the internet over which next-gen console is superior: the Xbox 360, the PS3 or the Wii. At times, the war has descended into name-calling and baseless finger-pointing. In the end, if you want to play Halo 3, get a 360. Like watching movies in some bullshit format? Go for the PS3. Wanna wave a controller around and pretend it's a tennis racquet? The Wii is your machine. Or, you know, you could go play tennis for real.

You can log out anytime you like, but you can never leave

These days, we're at a point where gamers could, conceivably, never leave the house again. Instead, they can kick back in an online role-playing game like World of Warcraft, where everyone thinks of you as a handsomely heroic knight in shining armour instead of a tragically greasy-haired creature in unwashed underpants. You can even make money from killing orcs and selling their gold to other players, then order your groceries online.

Lewd ludography

If the latest titles are any indication, reality is really going to have to lift its game. As soon as those tireless boffins perfect a USB sex simulator, the human race is doomed. After all, who would settle for that nice girl next door with the slightly crooked teeth when an army of physically perfect digital robobabes, dedicated solely to your pleasure, are only a mouseclick away? Especially if there's a high score table involved.

Finally, a way for nerds to exercise...

Man joins Socialist Alliance to pick up alternative chicks

NCIS fan and regular visitor to the Suicide Girls website Gary Bullock has admitted he only joined revolutionary political group Socialist Alliance on the chance that he "would meet some hot goth babes". Bullock, who cares nothing about the exchange of blood for oil and rides a Ducati motorbike, nevertheless agreed to sell copies of *Green Left Weekly* in a local mall "as long as that chick with the dreadlocks and neck tattoo shows me the ropes".

"I'm doing my bit for the oppressed and downtrodden of the world", said Bullock, pausing briefly to yell "G'day Sweeeetheart" at a passing blonde. "I bought a Che Guevara T-shirt and everything."

In response to a student newspaper questionnaire that asked how he would spend his day if he woke up as a woman, Bullock answered, "Smashing the glass ceiling, feeling the objectifying effect of the male gaze and playing with myself." He was quick to stress that the third response was intended to be an ironic play on sexist attitudes, and a celebration of female sexuality. "I consider myself a bit of a feminist – chicks should be allowed to vote and get paid the same as us, I reckon."

Citing his reasons for joining the Socialist Alliance as "the exploitation of Third World farmers, inequality of the West and an abundance of pierced nipples", Bullock has been warmly welcomed by his fellow revolutionaries, although he has failed to sleep with any of them as yet.

"Kris has got some great titties and she always wears a corset," he reported. "But she's all over Ben because he once spat on Michael Costa. I'm gonna invite her out for chai and vegan mudcake, to discuss Walter Benjamin's theories of art in the age of mechanical reproduction. Then I'll take her back to my place, where we'll watch *The Motorcycle Diaries* and maybe have a few drinks.

"If all goes well, I might even con her into giving me a blowie," he said. "In a way that's empowering for her."

Gary hopes a winning smile and his opposition to the war in Iraq will be enough to help him score

Jessica Fletcher charged with 689 murders

Popular mystery writer Jessica Fletcher has been charged with 689 homicides previously declared solved. Police say Fletcher concocted an image as a harmless busybody and amateur sleuth as a means of avoiding suspicion, allowing to kill her victims with means varying from a marble bust toppled from a roof-top to a rigged stunt man's gun. She avoided detection for many years, before prosecutors uncovered statistics showing Fletcher on or near the scene of hundreds of different homicides.

Cabot Cove, the sleepy Maine town the writer called home, was similar in size to nearby, violence-free towns, but suffered dozens of bloody murders in less than a decade. "It was just too much of a coincidence to ignore," FBI profiling expert John McDonald said. "A perpetrator offering to assist in the investigation of homicide they themself have committed is a pattern we often see in serial killings. The explanations for the crimes were just getting more and more improbable."

Fletcher was able to convince police she was genuine with a combination of homespun wisdom and plucky charm, even going as far as developing a relationship with the gruff but lovable local sheriff. "She was very convincing," said one investigator. "Her pat summation of the facts of the case, her uncanny ability to elicit a confession out of the least likely suspect, it was all very impressive. I mean, put her up against a crooked property developer trying to buy an old marina, and who are the cops going to believe?"

The FBI started to investigate Fletcher after receiving a tip-off from a cruise ship operator. "It got to the point where no cruise company would let her board one of their ships because they knew that as soon as she showed up, a corpse would soon follow," McDonald said.

Shakespearean actor Lionel Hitchens was one of those framed by the sociopathic widow. Despite protestations of innocence, he was led away in handcuffs after Fletcher gave a glib summation of his motives for a senseless crime. "Why would I kill another actor just because I was his understudy to play Hamlet? In an amateur theatre production? It didn't make any sense. But as soon as the police had spent a half-hour investigating it, they just went with the first explanation they heard, and didn't want to know any more."

While investigators say the evidence against Fletcher is overwhelming, they have not ruled out a surprise twist, possibly involving a surprise special guest star witness.

Fletcher with a friend she later falsely sent to the electric chair

Report card accurately predicts child's future

High school teachers have been revealed as Nostradamus-like prognosticators this month, with the report card of the then Year 9 student Jason Westwood describing exactly the sort of man he would become once he left school. Westwood, who found his old report in a plastic crate in his basement while looking for a bottle of bourbon he had hidden from his wife, described the commentary as "eerily prescient".

"Jason's work ethic is not what it could be. He has some aptitude, but his inability to do the set work means he often falls behind his peers." The comment was written by Padstow Primary School English teacher Jane Goodall in 1987, but it could just as easily have come from Westwood's supervisor some 20 years later, who often has to reprimand the accounts receivable clerk for his sloppy attention to detail.

"When I read the words, 'Jason has not displayed a positive attitude towards PE. He does very little in class and what he does do is inappropriate', it was like a mysterious voice from the past commenting on my inability to go to the gym regularly. Miss Brown might've been a detention-happy bitch, but she certainly nailed me on that one."

"And where she says in the end, I would only disappoint myself – bingo."

Further evidence of the high school staff's Cassandra-like powers came courtesy of Maths teacher Mr Porter's revelation

Westwood's latest report from his supervisor eerily mirrors his Year 9 one

that Jason "has no respect for his fellow students' learning", which uncannily predicted Westwood's future persona as the guy who is constantly trying to convince his co-workers to go out drinking on weeknights.

Westwood has vowed to show his old teachers they were wrong by making something of his life. "I'm gonna earn a million dollars on the stock market, then I'll go back and rub their faces in it," he said, fulfilling headmaster Mr Gunning's prophecy that he "has a head full of big ideas but cannot stick to anything."

Simone pours out heart to New Idea, Shane to new woman

Sally from Home & Away fears she may be typecast

DNA tests prove Larry Birkhead not responsible for Dannielyn's name

Scientists have conclusively established that Anna Nicole Smith's ex-boyfriend Larry Birkhead is the father of her child Dannielyn, and also exonerated him from any responsibility for choosing her name. Responsibility for the child's ungainly name will be determined by DNNNNA testing, and is thought to rest with Anna Nicole and, ultimately, her drug dealer.

"Anna was taking a lot of powerful depressants when she thought it up," her lawyer Howard K. Stern said. "And her memory will be kept alive when the name proves equally depressing for her daughter."

The testing has ended a period of frenzied media coverage, with Stern and a multitude of other men all claiming they may have been Dannielyn's father. "Who would have thought that Anna's reality television show would get even more macabre after she died?" one critic commented.

The newly-identified father said he was excited to be looking after his daughter, and even more excited to be looking after her immense fortune. As well as the money from the estate of oil tycoon J. Howard Marshall, Dannielyn has been granted ownership of her mother's primary assets, two enormous silicone breast implants.

"It's so sad that Anna isn't around to raise her daughter, but I will make sure she becomes the kind of woman her mother would have been proud of," Birkhead said. "One day Dannielyn too might take her clothes off for *Playboy* and marry an octogenarian oil billionaire for his money."

Stern said that the manner of Anna Nicole's death meant that his girlfriend-client had finally achieved her lifelong dream of emulating her heroine, Marilyn Monroe. "She achieved almost the same level of pin-up success," he said. "And her drug overdose followed by endless sordid sexual revelations has

Guilty of poor taste in women, not baby names

been even bigger than Marilyn's was.

"I just know that Anna would have died happy," he said. "If she hadn't been completely wasted."

Discovery of shallow grave ends eighteen-year search for Wally

The search for the missing adventurer popularly known as "Wally" may have come to a tragic conclusions, after police sectioned off an area of remote bushland Friday night. Detectives have since confirmed that a decomposed body has been located, and according to an unnamed source, the corpse was dressed in a faded, bloodstained red-and-white jumper, wearing round-rimmed glasses, and buried with a cane.

"The case has been especially difficult because of the mysterious nature of the victim," said police constable Darren Large. "We knew him as Wally, but according to Interpol he also went by aliases such as Waldo, Willy, Walter and Effy." False sightings in locations as various as Paris, Timbuktu and ancient Egypt also hampered the investigation.

Suspicion has once again fallen on self-described "arch-nemesis" Odlaw, and some investigators have also mooted the involvement of back-packer killer Ivan Milat. A sword-wielding Arab tribesman and a band of angry knights are also known to have carried grudges against Wally.

Wally's disappearance was something of a cause celebre in the early 1990s, when scores of volunteers joined the search for the traveller. The hunt was, at times, made problematic by the large number of people who looked and dressed like the missing man. Authorities took the unorthodox step of releasing books and TV shows filled with images of Wally, in the hopes of jogging someone's memory.

Wally is survived by fiancee Wanda, ex-girlfriend Wilma and dog Woof.

MISSING

**WALLY, AKA WALDO
Last seen in series of inexplicably popular children's books**

Kevin Rudd's Etiquette Guide
FOR THE MODERN UNION GENTLEMAN

The Hon Kevin Rudd M.P.
Leader of the Opposition

MEMO
FROM: Kevin Rudd
TO: Union Bosses

In order to counter the perception that the ALP is ruled by the unions, Greg Combet has told me to issue some new guidelines for acceptable behaviour by unionists.

These guidelines will apply to the activities of ALL union leaders:

- which is caught on video tape;
- up until the next election.

Please abide by these guidelines, or the media will force me to take strong action to prove my leadership credentials, an outcome we'd all prefer to avoid.

Pretty please.

Yours in solidarity (in principle only)

Kevin

TESTIMONIALS

"*Rudd's Etiquette Guide for the Modern Union Gentleman* cured me of my boorish ways and gave me the skills to deal with my knee-jerk expulsion from the Labor Party with charm and grace."

DEAN MIGHELL
Victorian State Secretary
Electrical Trades Union

"Thanks to *Rudd's Etiquette Guide for the Modern Union Gentleman*, now whenever I exercise my right of entry for OH&S inspections, I make sure to knock. And I never forget to send a thank you note!"

JOE MCDONALD
WA Assistant Secretary
Construction Forestry Mining and Energy Union

Being a union official is an important stage in the process of gaining pre-selection for the Australian Labor Party. Accordingly it is crucial that you adhere to the following rules of etiquette:

1. The gentleman unionist takes care to avoid foul language. Uncouth words such as "fuck", "shit", "poo", "boss", "strike", "scab", "working class", "socialism", "Left wing" and "Latham" are to be avoided in the presence of any recording device.

2. The gentleman unionist refrains from aggressive tactics which might affront the employer or deprive him of the superior bargaining power to which he is entitled.

3. The gentleman unionist does not gloat when his adversary makes a concession. If bestowed an overly generous wage increase, good manners dictate that he return any amount above CPI for fear of causing grievous offence in the salons to the likes of Messrs Akerman or Bolt.

4. The gentleman unionist avoids overly familiar behaviour in the presence of a lady, especially if she is Shadow Industrial Relations Minister. Prudence dictates that all encouters with such a lady should generally be attended by a chaperone from the office of the Leader of the Opposition.

5. The gentleman unionist makes donations to the political party of his choice in a discreet manner and without the expectation of public acclamation or private influence.

6. The gentleman unionist accepts offers of increased wages, however meagre, with good grace. Appearing ungrateful is the height of rudeness and may cause alarm to the financial markets, whose proclivity towards taking fright is to be heeded more than one's own interests.

7. To boast of one's power or influence, for example over the policies of a centrist political party, is churlish in the extreme and may cause the gentleman unionist to lose his place in polite society.

"Rudd's Etiquette Guide for the Modern Union Gentleman makes my job so much easier."

PETER SIMPSON
Employer

"Rudd's Etiquette Guide for the Modern Union Gentleman is fucking bullshit. Die scab dogs!"

KEVIN DANIELS
Picketer

Even Papuan cannibals find Naomi Robson tasteless

The West Papuan tribe at the centre of the Naomi Robson controversy has clarified that even though Naomi Robson was clearly possessed by malign spirits, they would not be willing to eat her. "Even if we did still eat humans, we don't like the taste of bile," an elder said.

Robson has defended herself from the allegations, saying that she had not been planning to save the child Wa-Wa from a potential ritualistic killing. "My make-up trucks would never make it into such a remote area," she said.

Despite being deported, the experience had some positive aspects for the *Today Tonight* crew, who were flattered to be told by the Indonesian government that they needed journalist visas.

"Apparently they were worried we might portray the Indonesian army as an oppressive force in West Papua," said one *Today Tonight* reporter. "But we explained that as long as they didn't move to Australia and open a dirty restaurant, they'd have nothing to worry about."

Nine's *60 Minutes* program has already rejected the story, but they say this was only because it was prohibitively expensive, and had not previously been covered by the BBC's *Panorama* program. "It was very expensive for just one boy threatened by cannibals," said a Nine spokesman. "If he was threatened by cannibals and also trapped down a mine, we might have considered it."

Robson and all the other Australian journalists have now returned home, to the great relief of Wa-Wa's tribe. "Frankly, between being victimised by tabloid journalists and cannibals, I'd take the cannibals," one elder said.

Robson returns from PNG with her cosmetics concierge

Chinese stock market regrets switching to Windows Vista

Peaking demand for commodities, investor jitters and competition with Japan have all been blamed for the recent Shanghai stock market crash, but now fingers are being pointed at a more familiar culprit – Microsoft software. Expecting a standard operating system, traders panicked when confronted with a series of ethereal, floating squares, a design one described as "even more wanky than a Mac, with none of the functionality."

The market looks set to recover slowly, as it is still installing updates for Internet Explorer, Windows Media Player and MSN Messenger, and their downloading is being blocked by a Windows security feature.

Microsoft has defended the product, which it claims is the most secure product it has ever produced. "Vista is a hundred times more secure than XP," said spokeswoman Amrita Singh, "and will be impervious to hackers for hours to come."

Singh also pointed out that while every other part of the program had failed, its "Experience Memories" function program worked perfectly. "Sure, Vista may have struggled under the weight of trading millions of stocks and bonds," said Singh, "but what about trading photos of a special moment with a loved one, or combining sounds and vision for a cool multimedia presentation that you don't have the right codec to watch?"

Singh then stated that Microsoft had now copyrighted both "trading photos of loved ones" and "cool multimedia presentations".

Some companies have been ambivalent about doing business with the communist Chinese regime, but Microsoft has had no reservations. "The Chinese love monopolies, hate competition, suppress dissenting views, abuse copyright and produce poorly made products – what's not to like?" said Singh.

Though he made significant losses, day trader Hong Leng ultimately concluded that the crisis at the Shanghai Stock Exchange could have been far worse. "I knew switching to Vista was a bad idea," he said. "I'm just glad it didn't trigger a regionwide financial meltdown, like when we installed Windows 98."

Traders desperately tried to switch off the tour of new features

Prince Harry disappointed Iraq's 'Green Zone' not what he thought

The hopes and dreams of the third in line to the British throne were dashed last month, when Prince Harry was cleared to fight in Iraq. The 22-year-old cornet had been keen to be posted in the region to "smoke some hash with the Arabs and chill out for a while". But Harry received a double blow when he learned not only that he would actually be required to patrol the Iranian border, but that Baghdad's famous "Green Zone" bore no resemblance whatsoever to Amsterdam's.

"I'm a goddamned prince of the realm," he said, fondling a socialite's breasts. "Why would I want to hang out with a bunch of stupid, classless inbreds with no idea about the real world? Other than ones with titles, I mean."

Harry calmed considerably after his Blues and Royals regiment were invited on a tour of Afghanistan's extensive poppy fields, even though his request for permission to sew a swastika onto his uniform "for a laugh" was denied.

The Prince is already undergoing combat training in a series of London nightspots, and said he is looking forward to the challenge. He will be the first royal to serve in combat since the Falklands, and the first to face beheading since Charles I.

The last British royal to see active duty was Prince Andrew, who flew helicopters in the Falklands War. "Don't make the same mistakes I did," he reportedly told his nephew. "Stay away from submarines, decoy missiles and racy, plump redheads."

Prince Harry has vowed to launch a drug offensive

Harry's father could not be reached for comment, although Prince Charles wished the young man well.

One-man attempt to start standing ovation unsuccessful

A concert-goer has tried and failed to single-handedly rouse his fellow audience members to a standing ovation. At the conclusion of an Australian Chamber Orchestra performance of Saint-Saëns' *Septet in E flat major*, Richard Worthstone, 57 of Neutral Bay, stood erect and clapped for a solid minute before turning, seeing no one else performing the same action, and finally resuming his seat.

The applause continued for several more minutes, leading Worthstone to make a second, shorter attempt to get the crowd on its feet. It was equally abortive.

"He had a pretty good shot at it," said Jessica Chan, also present. "He really made it look like he was enthused when he stayed up, instead of just trying to save face."

The self-described lover of the arts has previously tried to start standing ovations at the Sydney Theatre Company's production of *The Season at Sarsaparilla*, the ballet, and his own nephew's primary school Christmas pageant. His most successful attempt so far has garnered two followers.

"If you're sitting in the second or third row where most of the audience can see you, you've got a special responsibility," he said. "If anyone's going to start a standing ovation it's you. It's almost impossible to get a standing ovation going from the back row. Believe me – I've tried."

Worthstone denies that he has the manoeuvre on a hair trigger. "When I'm at a public event and feel genuinely moved, I like to express it," he said. "Australians can be quite hostile to elitism, but I applaud it. Whether that's by shouting 'bravis' at the

Worthstone the one time he convinced his wife to join him

opera, or counting in a Mexican wave at the cricket, it doesn't matter."

'BB' housemate Emma suspicious about new 'burying father' task

The producers of *Big Brother* have honoured a contestant's father's wish that his daughter Emma not be told of his death. "I've been watching the series, and I know how depressing the goings-on in that house are," he told family members. "I'm worried that the news could tip her over the edge."

Instead, all housemates will be allowed to share in the moment at a special, prime-time Friday Night Funeral episode. Mike Goldman, Bree Amer and Ryan Fitzgerald will conduct a moving service in the games arena. "They'll all have a chance to have a bit of fun with a shovel, and sling a bit of dirt around," Goldman said. "And as always with the prizes on Friday nights, the housemates won't know what's in the box."

BB producer Kris Noble says the producers are doing everything possible to handle the situation appropriately. He now intends to let viewers decide whether Emma should be told via a lucrative SMS poll.

The cat was nearly let out of the bag at last week's eviction show when an audience member held up a sign telling Emma that her father had died. Noble was quick to criticise the attempt to contact the housemate. "There couldn't be a more insensitive way to find out," Noble said. "We want to make sure the news is broken to her slowly and caringly. Surely there is no better way than being told by Gretel in a prime-time midweek special, once we've had time to run saturation advertising?"

Noble promised that when Emma is told, *BB's* in-house psychologist Carmel Hill would be on hand. "For the first time, she might have something worthwhile to contribute," he said.

A grief counsellor has criticised the producers, saying that the decision could cause major trauma to the contestant. But she later conceded that the harm would be minimal compared with the massive psychological damage done to Emma by being nationally famous for a month and then quickly returned to obscurity.

"They should break it to her that her father has died as soon as possible," she said. "And at the same time, they should break it to her that six months after leaving the house, her only regular celebrity appearances will be at Centrelink."

Emma... only a few months away from social death herself

The Chaser

Judge rules Paris Hilton is 'in' this season

A judge has ruled Paris Hilton will be "in" custody this season, sentencing her to 45 days in county jail. "Paris is known for her variety of looks," he said. "This season it'll be stripes."

The judge said he had considered a community service order instead of jail, but had decided that Hilton could best serve the community by being removed from it.

The heiress's case foundered after lawyers were unable to find any character witnesses, and instead used ignorance as a defence. "We thought we had a water-tight case," said attorney Howard Weitzman. "We argued that Paris knew nothing and that she hadn't done anything. Her entire career to date was our exhibit A."

Jail authorities recognise that Hilton will have special requirements as a prisoner. "There's a real risk of sexual assault, especially if she gets her hands on any Greek shipping heirs," prison overseer Captain Alice Scott said.

But Scott says she will get no special treatment. "We don't care if the uniform is a 'totally gross colour', and there's no way she's getting 24-hour access to the conjugal visits trailer."

E! has announced they will be capturing Paris' prison experience on camera, for season five of *The Simple Life*. "We're looking forward to filming Paris in a variety of prison-specific 'fish out of water' situations, like communal showering, fending off butch lesbians and hiding her Dior washcloth from fellow inmates."

The star has already gone on a hunger strike to protest her custodial sentence, and friend Nicole Richie has been refusing to eat solid food since Hilton's initial arrest in September 2006. The heiress says she is willing to accept some form of punishment, but has asked that the sentence be commuted to hotel detention.

Like many stars, Paris may be given community service on LA's freeways

KNOW YOUR ENEMY

BUSES

Compared to buses, trains are a godsend. Sure, the trip takes longer and you're stuck with a carriage of disease-carrying arseholes till you arrive at your stop, but nothing beats crowded inner-city buses for sheer commuting awfulness. Here's a selection of fellow passengers to watch out for.

HOMELESS PEOPLE: They may have a mental illness and be down on their luck, victims of an uncaring society where not all are treated equally, but does that mean they have to sit directly behind me, smelling of faeces, calling the police and telling them, "I'm about to be assaulted" when there's no one else around but me? And where the hell are they going, anyway?

SEAT HOGS: It's always the corporate dorks in their suits. They resent having to share their seat with anyone, so they try to make it look like they need the whole thing and pretend to be fully absorbed with their mp3 player and important SMS work. If you sit next to one of these overly aftershaved pricks, prepare to engage in a trip-long passive-aggressive war for territory, where the seat hog will keep their legs open, shoulders back and arms to the side. Also, he'll never get off the bus before you do.

BACK-SEAT BANDITOS: These guys are either in high school, or still wish they were. You can spot them a bus length away – having paid the fare they stride up the aisle, heads full of memories of the time they fingered that Year 9 chick behind the canteen, and flop down in the centre of the back seat. This makes it difficult for anyone to take one of the other four spots back there, unless they're of a similar mindset to the first guy. The end result's the same – a pack of morons manning the emergency push-out window.

SHOPPERS: Space is a premium on the bus, and the jerks who get on at peak hour with arms full of David Jones and Peter Alexander bags laden with the fanciest in wardrobe technology don't help matters. Honestly, if you have the means to spend thousands of dollars on frilly silk dresses, then you can afford to catch a cunting cab. Don't flop down in the front seats reserved for the elderly, taking up the space of four men with your exciting purchases, then act like you can't see the pregnant woman standing in the aisle.

GALLANTRY ISSUES: This may be your biggest foe on the bus, especially if you're a young man with no visible handicaps. Personally, I take a deeply hypocritical view, where if I'm standing I like to glare balefully at anyone who doesn't give up their seat for a lady, but if I'm sitting down I come over all opportunistically feminist and unaware of the world outside my magazine and mp3 player.

Also, if there's an old person I pretend I don't see them, rationalising that I've been at work all day, my back gets sore if I stand up for too long and besides, I paid full price for my ticket and they got a pensioner discount. That old bitch should've stayed at home knitting doilies and wishing her daughter would visit. It's not my fault her hips don't work as well as they used to. As you can see, chivalry's a thorny issue in these modern times.

2007

BEN COUSINS
REHAB DIARY

Day 1: Was stopped at rehab gate and asked if I had any booze. Left the car and did a runner. Daniel Kerr reckons I should have smashed them.

Day 3: Stopped running.

Day 5: Went for my first run in rehab. Received standing ovation for everything I've overcome.

Day 7: They say drugs remain in your hair for months. I don't care what they say no one's touching my mullet!

Notes

Day 8: Was told to have a long hard look at myself. Like what I see.

Day 9: Had a great massage. They used two bottles of massage oil on my arms almost as much as I use during games!

Day 10: Had my first group support session. Got my Dad to make a statement on my behalf. He received a standing ovation for everything he's overcome.

Day 12: Was introduced to my specialist today. He spent entire session asking me to say hi to other Eagles players for him.

Notes

Day 15: All this vego shit is making me spew even more than I do on the ground.

Day 17: Discovered my room has a mini-bar! Was going to stay away from the grog but then remembered the Eagles are picking up the tab. Sweet!

Day 19: Just read a Robert Walls column bagging me out. Received a standing ovation for overcoming even more.

Day 21: Had a hydration session. Doctor asked me how much I drank per day. This time I smashed him. Kerr's right, it worked a treat.

Notes

Day 24: Standing ovation went way too long today, but I overcame the tedium. Earnt myself another standing ovation.

Day 25: Therapist forced me to confront some ugly home truths. Thankfully an Eagles spokesperson stepped in and cleared things up with a blanket denial.

Day 27: Here everyone is treated exactly the same. It's really been a wake-up call. Never leaving Perth again.

Day 28: Cured. Off to the Burswood Casino to celebrate.

Orkopoulos pleads 'respect my 30 presumptions of innocence'

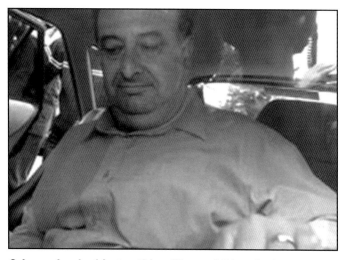

Orkopoulos looking nothing like a child molester

Warning: Former NSW Aboriginal Affairs Minister Milton Orkopoulos is currently facing criminal charges and has not yet been convicted. To ensure that he gets a fair trial, you should only read this article if you already think he's guilty.

The former NSW Labor Minister Milton Orkopoulos has reminded the public that he should be presumed innocent of each of the 30 separate child sex and drug offences he was charged with in Newcastle this week. "I do not want to be subjected to trial by media," Mr Orkopoulos said in thirty press releases the day after he was charged. "In fact I'm quite keen to avoid a trial of any sort."

"I'd especially like you to presume I'm innocent of the child prostitution charge,"

Mr Orkopoulos added. "And if you could still presume me to be innocent even after the evidence against me is presented, that would be great too." Orkopoulos denies all the charges, and has vowed to spend the upcoming months "preparing my legal defence and enjoying my freedom".

A defiant NSW Premier Morris Iemma said the charges against Mr Orkopoulos "will not distract me from the business of government, most of which involves sacking other Ministers."

The Premier said he would take a strong law and order platform to the next election, pledging to stamp out sex crime, drug use, consorting with prostitutes and dangerous driving, "and that's just in my Cabinet".

Panama hat salesman resigns after admitting he met Brian Burke

Perth's leading Panama hat salesman has resigned after admitting business dealings with his one and only customer, former Western Australian Premier Brian Burke. "In this line of work, all my business dealings are supposed to be shady," he said. "But when Mr Burke brought Kevin Rudd into the shop to try on some hats, I knew I was fatally compromised."

But the salesman is adamant that Mr Rudd did not himself purchase a panama hat. "He wasn't interested in anything that might stop his face being in the media spotlight," he explained.

The scandal over Mr Burke's contacts has already led to the resignation of four members of the WA Labor government, as well as Mr Burke's wife and entire family.

The controversy has left inexperienced Premier Alan Carpenter with no choice but to seek advice on how to the resolve the crisis from Mr Burke. Police listening in to the Premier's telephone calls with Mr Burke say it was he who decided that any MPs dealing with him should be sacked.

Mr Burke's latest victim is philosophical about having to

Lecter – the second most evil panama hat fan

leave his job. "To be honest, it's not much of a loss to be getting out of the panama hat game. Brian's fashion choices haven't exactly been great for sales. My mafia clients have returned their hats: not even they want to be associated with Burke."

But he admits the scandal has affected him. "After all this contact with Brian Burke, my reputation is totally shattered. In fact the only person I can get a reference from is Kelvin Thompson."

Strip club proves to be less classy than ad promised

Visitors to Wollongong's Moulin Bleu gentleman's club have confessed to being disappointed by the ambience and décor of the venue, having been led to believe the place catered to a more sophisticated clientele. "The posters out the front conjured up images of tasteful European erotica and ribald burlesquery," said patron Oliver Barron. "They didn't say anything about the tacky modern art prints or cheap carpet that's obviously designed to hide vomit stains."

Despite claiming to possess "a touch of Parisian elegance", the club's main features appear to be dim lighting, aggressive security guards and naked blonde women with breast implants swinging on poles in exchange for money.

"I ordered a Campari and soda," said punter Lionel Cuthbert, "and the barman told me they only serve VB and cask wine. I can't believe I dressed up for this. I feel a bit bloody stupid in this tie and jacket, I can tell you."

Although Moulin Bleu manager Vinnie Theroux boasts that he has spent over $150,000 on fibre optic lights for the entrance and "had the upholstery fully replaced with maroon leather", both patrons and exotic dancers agree he has failed to bring a shred of glamour to the strip club.

"When I saw the job ad in the paper, I was picturing myself as Natalie Portman in *Closer*," said stripper Tracy "Absinthe" Atkinson. "In this dive, I feel more like Elizabeth Berkley in *Showgirls*."

Theroux is planning a complete renovation of the club, to give it more of an Ancient Roman feel. "It'll be classy," he said. "You know, with grapes and orgies and shit."

The Moulin Bleu, where taking your clothes off for money is just... taking your clothes off for money

Text message lacks nuance

Critics have slammed an SMS sent by account executive Morgan Teuber to a group of his friends, claiming the tone of his brief communication is unclear. The text message, which stated a desire "2 C TRANSFORMERS ITLL B COOL", has divided recipients, who are unable to reach consensus on whether Teuber was serious, joking or something else entirely.

"I'm not sure what to write back," said SMS receiver Karen Hite. "Both 'lol yeah right' and 'how about thurs nite?' are problematic, given that I'm not sure what he's is trying to say. I don't want to enthusiastically agree and look like an idiot...but on the other hand, I don't want to make a joke about it and hurt Morgan's feelings if he really does want to see *Transformers*."

Compounding her confusion is the fact Teuber wrote his message entirely in capital letters, giving the impression he is yelling. "On second thoughts, it's probably safer not to reply at all," she said.

According to sociology professor Marcus Jackson, these conundrums are all too common: "Unfortunately, it is well-nigh impossible to accurately convey tone or inflection via SMS. Especially when the sender refuses to make use of smileys, acronyms or multiple exclamation marks."

Teuber's text message has renewed calls for a nationally standardised instant-messaging grammar, with visual cues allowing recipients to immediately identify jokes, anger and genuine interest in watching live-action cinematic remakes of 1980s cartoons.

Karen tries to craft a meaningful response to the inpenetrable SMS

"It's getting out of hand," said Shadow Communications Minister Stephen Conroy. "Under the current system, we cannot definitively know whether someone is being sarcastic, or whether they legitimately want us to kiss their balls."

CLUEDO®
Channel Nine edition
9

Who killed Kerry Packer's top-rating television network? Was it Jessica Rowe on the *Today Show* Set with her inane laugh? Or was it James Packer in the PBL Boardroom with a corporate takeover? With Channel Nine Cluedo, you can play Gerald Stone in the comfort of your own home!

TODAY SHOW SET

PBL BOARDROOM

CHURCH OF SCIENTOLOGY

THE CATCH-UP COUCH

EDDIE'S OFFICE

NATIONAL NINE NEWSROOM

QUIZMANIA SWITCHBOARD

TONY GREIG'S WAREHOUSE OF CRAP CRICKET MEMORABILIA

BURKE'S BACKYARD

THE SUSPECTS

REV ALEXANDER — DID HIS EFFICIENCY DRIVE DOWNSIZE PROFIT AS WELL?

MS ROWE — WAS SHE THE LAUGHING ASSASSIN?

PROFESSOR McGUIRE — DID EDDIE EVERYWHERE TAKE THE NETWORK NOWHERE?

MR PACKER — DID HIS FOCUS ON GAMBLING LEAVE NINE DOUBLE DOWN?

MS GRIMSHAW — DEATH BY BOTOX?

COLONEL LECKIE — A REVENGE KILLING BY THE SEVEN BOSS ON THE NETWORK THAT SACKED HIM?

MURDER WEAPONS

Private equity selloff

Humiliating appearance on Kerri-Anne

Chequebook journalism

Alan Jones

Bone

Bert's toupée

Football rights

51

Why do you think Kevin Rudd is polling well?

"I have a very strong approval of Kevin Rudd – as Opposition Leader."

"I'm very susceptible to advertising, so Rudd has impressed me. And so has the Nando's stripper."

"You can't place any store in early polls. The Australian people in their own time and space will determine how they feel about the current government and whether they want to endorse it in the future."

"Sorry, is he leading the Labor party? My mistake."

"I simply wouldn't consider a person who is only three times as popular as Simon Crean to be 'polling well'."

"Sorry if I appeared a little brusque before. I just didn't wish to appear as if I was jumping the gun, so to speak, or counting my eggs, as it were. I very much appreciated the chance to weigh in on this pertinent and contentious issue."

"Rudd said he'd personally make the case to every Australian why they should vote for him. And I think most Australians are anxious to avoid that conversation."

"Fancy bumping into you again. Has it already been five minutes? It seems like yesterday. Well, I won't keep you. If you need anything more, I'll be around, just helping some Australians."

"Rudd has impressed me in the campaign so far. Although I'm keen to know more about what 'Don't Know' has to say."

"The Government seems stale and arrogant. It's time for someone fresh and arrogant to have a go."

"Sorry just one more thing   wondering when you might next be around here gathering vox pops? Just in case I have something further to add on any particular issue. You've got my phone number? Just in case, it's 0409 112 111. Good bye."

"That's 0409 112 111. I'd better get yours too."

The Chaser

Rushdie delighted by knighthood: seeks armour

Author Salman Rushdie has gratefully received the honour of a knighthood, and is now looking forward to the protective measures that accompany it. The novelist has already asked if he can keep the guard of honour that accompanied him to the ceremony. "I know I've been critical of pomp and ceremony in the past," he said. "But I've come to appreciate some of the most ancient aspects of knighthood, like carrying a shield everywhere, and constantly praying for protection."

Rushdie said he was pleased to have his efforts recognised rather than his face, and will use the opportunity the award presents to try and stay alive for a little while longer.

Not surprisingly, the knighthood has provoked a storm of fury from the Islamic world. Pakistan called the Queen's representative to Islamabad, to explain himself and model for an effigy, while an angry Tehran said they were willing to try and defuse the situation.

"We could reach a compromise position," said the Iranian ambassador. "where we keep the part of the ceremony where Rushdie kneels and a sword is produced, and just change the ending."

Rushdie – bringing down the establishment from within

Pakistani clerics responded in kind by giving terrorist mastermind Osama Bin Laden their highest possible honour – he will now throw the opening pitch at the Islamist World Series baseball game.

Outgoing Prime Minister Tony Blair was said to be surprised at the furore, claiming that many of the people objecting to the award "hadn't even read *The Satanic Verses*. And I'm not surprised," he added. "It's completely unintelligible."

He also denied that the action was inflammatory to Muslims, but agreed it could be inflammatory to Glasgow airport.

SPOTLIGHT ON:

BIKIE GANGS

HELLS ANGELS
★ Links to nightclubs, narcotics, prostitution, and last week's tragic shooting in Melbourne.
★ Vicious. Approach with caution.

MID-LIFE MOFO'S
★ Overweight CEO's fulfilling teenage fantasies on expensive bikes – No criminal connections
★ Generally harmless but could crush you in the boardroom.

VESPA VILLAINS
★ Links to cafés, small galleries, etc.
★ Top speed 70 km/hr
★ Grouchy before morning espresso.

Pub trivia champ humiliated on 'Temptation' quiz show

Despite regularly winning the Thursday night trivia at his local watering hole, history buff Gerald Sugden failed to answer a single question correctly during his one-night stint on the Nine Network's *Temptation*. Viewers say Sugden occasionally attempted to press his buzzer, but for the most part sat silently, with an intense look of sweaty, baffled concentration.

"I don't know what happened," said Sugden, who read *The Really Difficult Quiz Book* and played countless games of Trivial Pursuit in preparation for the show. "My team, The Dukes of Ale, always take home the $50 drink voucher at Trivia Madness! down at the Oxford, so I thought I'd be a real contender on *Temptation*.

"Jesus, I was already spending the Vault money."

According to his wife Cassandra, Sugden's problems began almost as soon as he sat down. "I could tell Gerald was nervous," she said. "When Ed and Livinia asked him about his Franklin Mint collection, he just froze, then mumbled something about passing them on to our kids.

"We don't even have kids," she added.

Things only got worse for Sugden, who mistakenly thought Matthew Flinders discovered Tasmania and took no part in the tense, neck-and-neck race through the final fast money round that led to the carryover champ narrowly retaining her crown. "I can't believe I memorised all the Melbourne Cup winners and Soviet leaders," said Sugden. "I thought for sure there'd be something on Makybe Diva, what with the equine flu and everything."

"I'm glad the smug bastard lost," said fellow pub trivia attendee Rob Clifford, of the Pint Professors. "The look on his stupid, fat, I-know-all-about-the-Russian-Revolution face when he realised the only thing he was taking home was a pen was priceless. Maybe it'll stop him trying to correct the quizmaster's pronunciation for a week or two."

"I thought Gerald would at least get a pick of the board," said fellow Duke of Ale Harry Dell. "He knew the answer to the first fame game was Ike Turner – we had a similar question at the pub two weeks ago. Why he said 'Ted Mulry' instead, I'll never know."

"One thing's for sure – he's definitely not holding the pen this Thursday."

'Temptation' host Ed Phillips asks yet another question Gerald was unable to answer

Marcel Marceau eulogist at a loss for words

Bob Brown opens 'progressive' Bebo account

Always one step ahead of his political counterparts, Greens senator Bob Brown has joined social networking site Bebo, setting up an account under the name 'Greenblooded'. "While other politicians go for the glitz and glamour of MySpace or the slick, corporate look of Facebook," he said in the 'Me, My Life And I' section of his profile, "I chose an environmentally conscious alternative."

Although Senator Brown's primary reason for setting up the Bebo account is to connect with the voters of Australia, he has also used the opportunity to make contact with some of his heroes. "I have a friend request pending with Al Gore," he said. "I really want to tell him how much I enjoyed *An Inconvenient Truth*."

Visitors to Brown's profile can not only read up on the senator's current policy initatives and political beliefs, but also learn that his favourite band is Rush and he likes cowboy movies, as well as seeing the extent to which he is looking forward to reading the next Harry Potter book.

"It's great to see international leaders using our site as a platform to speak to the public," said Bebo founder Michael Birch. "It's exactly the kind of thing I had in mind when I came up with the Widget application."

Brown in a rare moment of offline communication

Brown is quick to sing the praises of the website: "I've always been a fan of direct democracy, and Bebo offers instant feedback from the public on my humanitarian legislation ideas and amateur photography. Besides which, it doesn't kill as many trees as how-to-vote cards and ballot papers do. My only complaint with the site is that my first account name choice, 'Green4Life', was already taken."

According to his profile's 'What are you doing?' status, Brown has been "working on a three-year plan to ban coal imports and listening to Rush's classic *2112*".

Man yet to find situation not covered by 'Simpsons' quote

Whether he's informing his wife she's a 'big, fat dynamo' or telling his co-workers not to 'have a cow, man', Brisbane removalist Gareth Schreiber takes all his conversational cues from *The Simpsons*. The 32-year-old, who has been watching the long-running TV show since it began, is able to apply his encyclopaedic knowledge of the program to any circumstance, be it a deceptively painful injury or a discussion on the relative cowardice of the French.

"No matter what wacky situation life throws at me," he said, "I always know I can look to Homer, Bart or Chief Wiggum for inspiration. If I'm telling my missus why I love her, I can say 'It's not just the sex – it's also the food preparation.' Seeing a solar eclipse, 'My eyes – zee goggles do nothing!' Eating a Mars Bar, 'Mmm… chocolate.' You could say this play has everything! As Mr Burns would tell you, it's…excellent."

According to experts, Schreiber is not alone. In the past, people would turn to Shakespeare or the Bible in search of a pithy turn of phrase but today, more and more discerning commercial TV viewers are referring to Matt Groening as 'Bard Simpson'. Chris Turner, author of *Planet Simpson*, explained: "*The Simpsons* has a breadth and longevity not found in other contemporary cartoons like *South Park* or *Family Guy*, or even live-action works like *Two And A Half Men* or *The Cherry Orchard*. Honestly, where else would you find such poignant moments of genius as the time Mr Burns' lost innocence was symbolised by the loss of his teddy bear?"

Gareth and his family prepare for a fancy dress party

Not everyone shares Schreiber's enthusiasm for *The Simpsons*, however. Some find his incessant repetition of "Hi-diddly-ho" and "Thank you, come again" irritating. Among these critics is his boss Adam Phelps: "Hearing Gareth yada yada yada about that show makes me wanna scream 'SERENITY NOW!'

"He's a close-talking hipster doofus," he said. "Not that there's anything wrong with that."

But Schreiber remains unperturbed. "Hens love roosters, geese love ganders, everyone else loves *Simpsons* quotes. Except my boss," he said. "So, everyone who counts loves *Simpsons* quotes."

Howard YouTube video secures key bored secretary vote

John Howard has released his first video on YouTube, providing much-needed diversion for the bored office workers whose votes he needs to win this year's election. The Prime Minister is delighted that he has managed to produce something that has received a better response from low-income workers than WorkChoices.

"The video had some novelty value," said administrative assistant and office YouTube addict Mike Withers, who is known on the site as "madman_m1ke". "But if he really wants us to forward it to all of our friends, he needs to spice things up a little," he advised. "Maybe he could make his announcements while playing the Tetris theme on the piano, or cut in a bit of footage of humping animals."

Withers has promised that if Howard makes his next policy announcement while doing tricks on a skateboard, he has his support. "Not just my vote in the election," he said. "But more importantly for my favourite videos list."

The Liberal Party President, Brian Loughnane, says he has been encouraging the Prime Minister to embrace new technology to try and win a new audience. "I wanted him to own this new medium with a fresh, funky clip that showed punters he's still with it after all these years," he said. "But he wanted to record a detailed, technical defence of his climate change record. Oh well, maybe next time we'll put some hip-hop music in the intro or something."

Howard's opponent Kevin Rudd has been faster to embrace the popular video-sharing

Howard hopes to equal the grassroots appeal of a skateboarding dog

site, having posted dozens of clips that have attracted tens of thousands of hits. But an insider at YouTube has revealed that nearly all of those hits came from the Labor leader's own computer.

YouTube, which has become a major player in US politics and is currently

hosting several online debates between the leading Presidential candidates, was initially eager for its site to become the home of Australian political videos as well. But after viewing Howard's initial effort, the company's management has quietly abandoned the idea.

59

Blair exit ends 28 years of conservative rule

After having to live with conservative prime ministers for nearly 30 years, British liberals are hoping Tony Blair's retirement will give their nation its first left-wing government in decades and a return to the glory days of Harold Wilson. "We're all holding our breath," said Labour voter Eric Cudlipp. "Maybe now we'll see some power returned to trade unions, welfare reform and a government that isn't in lockstep with Republican warmongers."

Other voters on the progressive side of politics are more cautious, remembering the brief resurgence of hope they experienced in 1997, when the Conservative Party was voted out of office. "At first, Blair looked like one of us, what with introducing the minimum wage and providing extra benefits to pensioners," one unionist said. "But then he started privatising and slashing everything and slashing welfare, and we realised that 'New Labour' was basically the same as 'Old Tory'."

"I am very proud of the legacy I will leave behind," said Blair. "Future generations will remember me not only as the man who coined the phrase 'people's princess' and introduced unprecedented levels of civilian surveillance, but also as the only British prime minister to appear on an episode of *The Simpsons*."

Blair's term continued the policy trends of political peers Thatcher and Major, as well as maintaining a steady stream of government-rocking bedroom scandals. From the erosion of civil liberties and welfare cuts to affairs with secretaries and sexed-up reports on Saddam Hussein's ownership of WMDs, his New Labour has been a bastion of efficient, rational right-wing government.

Former opposition leader Iain Duncan Smith has paid tribute to the outgoing leader: "We couldn't touch him. Every time we brought out a policy, he'd go one better. We said we'd restore Britain to her days of empire-building glory; he invaded Iraq."

Blair's anointed successor Gordon Brown is looking forward to taking office, and also to leaving it shortly afterwards.

Tony Blair bares his teeth for the first and last time

The Chaser

Everybody hates Kyle

Kyle Sandilands' one talent is making people hate him. But it's a gift he has in spades.
After yet another year of constant feuding, we have compiled the most definitive list yet of everyone who does.

Marcia Hines
As she regularly proves on *Idol*, she's incapable of disliking anyone at all ever – but if she hated someone, it would be Kyle.

Dave Hughes
Hates him because he's also a made it as a successful breakfast radio host, but without ever saying anything funny.

Jackie O
Spends three hours in his company each morning. Enough said.

Justin Timberlake
Hates him for spoiling designer beards for everyone.

Howard Stern
Hates him because Kyle is also always described as a "shock jock".

Ian 'Dicko' Dickson
Hates him for showing that anyone can be the arsehole judge on *Idol*.

Andrew Denton
Hates him because interviewing him for *Enough Rope* meant having to speak to him.

Mike Carlton

Hates him even more than he hated Stan Zemanek.

Andrew G

Hates him because there's only room for one vain, obnoxious blond on the set of Idol.

Kyle Sandilands

Knows he ought to punch himself in the throat.

2Day FM listeners

Hate him so much that their rage compels them to listen to him every morning.

Professor Stanley Withers

As Head of Singing at the Conservatorium of Music, he has been expertly judging musical talent for over 20 years. But he was overlooked as a judge for *Australian Idol* in favour of some preening, self-promoting blowhard whose idea of musical criticism is to abuse someone for their loose upper arms.

Tamara Jaber

Despite being his girlfriend, she hates him for signing her to King Kyle Records. Yes, that is the actual name of his record label.

Planet Earth

Just plain hates him.

Frenzal Rhomb

Partly hates him because of the fight they had over that concert, but mainly hates him for getting ten times Jay & The Doctor's ratings.

Kyle from South Park

Absolutely hates having the same name, despite being a fictional character.

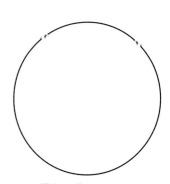

Blank space

(Write your reason for despising Kyle above.)

Bush and Howard now closer than ever: in polls

Embattled President George W. Bush says he now values John Howard's friendship more than ever. "After all these years, John and I find ourselves in a similar situation," he said during a joint press conference at APEC. "I'm prevented from being re-elected by the US Constitution, and he's prevented by public opinion.

"We were together on Iraq, we were together on global warming," he said. "And now we're together under the massive backlash from those policies. It was a bonding experience.

"Besides, I think anyone would appreciate John's friendship if the only other person who hadn't abandoned them was Dick Cheney."

John Howard said he was glad to be hosting his good friend again. "It's great to have him here, even if he had to decline my invitation to stay at Kirribilli House, citing 'security concerns'. I guess I was thinking that since Laura isn't here, perhaps we could hang out, watch a few videos and maybe sink a few cold ones. But of course I understand he's a very busy man. Free worlds don't lead themselves."

The Prime Minister dismissed the idea that his closeness to the President may be hurting him politically. "I'm sticking by George Bush because he's a mate. And when someone's your mate, that's for life," he said. "And I hope the President remembers that when I lose the election."

Despite his enormous admiration for Bush, the Prime Minister drew the line at accepting the President's offer of last-minute campaign help from another of his close friends, Karl Rove.

Although it seems the two will never be close friends, President Bush is nevertheless planning to strike up a cordial relationship with Kevin Rudd when they meet at APEC. He is particularly eager to obtain tips from the Opposition Leader on how he can perform so well in the polls despite holding almost identical positions to Howard.

Howard and Bush: together alone

Kevin Andrews' Case Against Haneef

* Dark skin
* First name is Mohamed
* Second cousins implicated in Glasgow Airport bombings
* Owns a SIM card that was found inside one of the cars
* Owns a SIM card from Optus – reception was VERY suss
* Only had old, dog-eared copies of 'New Idea' in his waiting room
* Worked in Queensland, just like that other dodgy Indian doctor
* Left the country when deported
* Wants to come back
* Collingwood fan
* Locked up for a long time without being charged – just like David Hicks
* Failed character test
* Kevin Andrews doesn't like him
* Peter Beattie does like him
* Better to be safe than sorry
* Laughed during 'Norbit'

* We have evidence that would totally convince you. Promise. But we can't release it because it would hinder other investigations.
* Has been known to leave toilet seat up
* He might be a terrorist
* Yeah? Well you prove he isn't

Anna Nicole Smith: golddigger now seeking gravedigger

Actress and TrimSpa spokeswoman Anna Nicole Smith's legal battle has died at the age of 39DD. The star has left behind one daughter, one stalker/lawyer and eighteen frivolous lawsuits. "It's comforting to know that Anna Nicole died doing what she loved," said a close friend. "The Bahamian Immigration Minister, apparently."

Tributes have poured in from fellow celebrities and adolescent boys all over the world. "I had a lot of time for Anna Nicole," said close friend Hugh Hefner. "Specifically 8.30-9.00pm on Fridays.

"I hope that wherever she is, she's at peace. Washing a car, or in front of a fire somewhere, wearing a diaphanous lacy top or something. Excuse me."

As many as three men have claimed to be father of Smith's daughter, Dannielynn, with Tony Abbott's involvement yet to be ruled out. But the star's will left her $400 million estate to her deceased son, cutting out her lawyer, confidante and possible murderer, Howard K. Stern.

"Didn't my following her around, smelling her hair for a decade mean anything?" said the embittered lawyer. "It's like the love, affection and free methadone were all for nothing."

Despite the snub, Stern is still in charge of planning the funeral, and plans to use the same embalmer who worked on Smith's son, stepson and former husband J. Howard Marshall, the latter while he was still alive.

The lawyer is also penning a eulogy that compares Anna Nicole to Marilyn Monroe a minimum of five times. He will deliver it incoherently himself while partially disrobed, before being removed from the moving ceremony by ushers.

The former Playmate's fans have requested an open casket.

Anna Nicole Smith in a happier stupor

Rumsfeld finally reveals his exit strategy

America's war in Iraq has claimed its most popular casualty yet, Donald Rumsfeld, who has announced his resignation. Rumsfeld denied that he was "cutting and running" from the challenges of office, saying his resignation was a "phased withdrawal" from the Secretariat.

His likely successor, Bob Gates, says he will focus more on metrics, identifying key numbers that can be used to measure the war's progress. "The first number we're looking at is the number of people called 'Donald Rumsfeld' working in the Pentagon," said Gates. "We hope to reduce it to zero."

The President expressed full confidence in Rumsfeld only days ago, and few saw the SecDec's imminent departure coming. Least of all Rumsfeld who became suspicious only when he caught Karl Rove practising his signature. The final decision to leave came only after Bush asked him to go hunting with Vice President Dick Cheney.

Rumsfeld leaves behind a mixed legacy. He was both the youngest and the oldest Secretary of Defense ever; the most self-confident and the most incompetent. He simultaneously cut troop numbers and committed US Forces to two wars, an innovation he called "supply side deployment."

Some woes look set to follow him out of office, with news that a human rights group is seeking to prosecute him in Germany over alleged war crimes at Abu Ghraib. "I'm confident these charges are baseless," says Rumsfeld. "Fallujah – they might be onto something. But these abuse allegations will be easier to beat than a manacled Iraqi boy."

True to form, he has made no plans for retirement, or for anything else, merely confidently predicting that the corporate sector will welcome him with "garlands of flowers". But observers say he may be able to bring his torture expertise to the private sector. "I predict he'll just keep doing the same thing he's been doing for many years now," one insider commented. "And that's making money for Halliburton."

Rumsfeld – cried like a little girl

NO -THAT'S MY NUTSACK.

anWeldon.

JANUARY

"January – don't be mad, don't be angry to me." So sang Pilot, and with good cause. No matter what time of year it is, you can always count on another Janus-faced month looming darkly in the future, waiting to make a mockery of all the hopes, dreams and achievements you entertained the year before. It's a vile, garnet and carnation-loving 31-day period that delivers none of the exquisite delights promised by festive December. Here are some pitfalls to look out for in January – the worst month of the year.

BROKEN RESOLUTIONS: All it takes is one tipple, cigarette or chocolate mudcake and you find yourself in the hell paved by the road of your good intentions. Those few minutes after midnight on the cusp of New Year's Eve and New Year's Day are a wellspring of hope and commitment to a new way of life – and by the time mid-January rolls round, it has all been decimated. The best thing to do is resolve something petty and achievable, like "I will not drink Melbourne Bitter unless there's no other booze in the house."

END OF THE HOLIDAYS: Speaking of fresh starts, you'll find yourself back at work after a well-deserved holiday. Rested and calm, you'll approach the challenges of your career with a keen eye and a 'can do' attitude – for around half of the first day back. It only takes four hours for the suffocating veil of routine to settle onto your consciousness – fluorescent office lights blot out the holiday goodwill even faster than they fade a summer tan.

AUSTRALIA DAY: Barbecues, beer and backyard cricket. It sounds like good fun, but no one mentions blowflies, sunburn and the pretence at patriotism, do they? Worst of all, there's the crushing disappointment of listening to Triple J's Hottest 100 and realising you hate almost every song venerated by pseudo-rebellious teenagers the year before. This is a train of thought that can, sadly, only lead to 2Day FM, classic hits or John Laws.

CHRISTMAS DEBT: Yule seems like an age ago when the bills start rolling in. All that savings-dwindling and charging it you did in a Tasmanian Devilish whir of celebratory goodwill to all men and other family members looks pretty stupid in the cold, hard light of January. Especially since the assortment of *Chaser Annuals* and Hottest 100 CDs you received will never justify the amount you spent on glossy hardcover cookbooks, electrical appliances, and house and land packages for your friends and family.

WRITING THE WRONG DATE ON THINGS: This also serves to remind you that a year you thought was in the recent past was actually a decade ago. If you're an adult, you'll recall how cranky with yourself you'd get for writing the wrong year in your schoolbooks... and this will cause you to ruminate on how long ago that actually was. Plus, it's a pain if you're trying to post-date cheques.

Lost mountain-climber already envisioning book deal

Danish tourist Nikolaj Neilsen, who has been lost in the Snowy Mountains for seven days, is already imagining a successful and profitable publishing career once he is rescued. The 23-year-old fell 35 metres when a rope snapped, causing him serious injury. "I've been keeping a video diary," he said, sheltering under an icy overhang. "I plan to use it as a reference when I recount my harrowing experience in a gripping tale of tenacity and survival for a major publisher."

Although he is delirious from a lack of food and loss of blood, Neilsen has managed to keep his spirits up: "The only thing that's kept me going, despite my frostbitten leg and broken arm, is the thought of all the inspirational talks I can give at universities and schools. Picturing their awed faces as I share my brave story almost makes having to drink my own urine worthwhile.

"I might even get to meet Ray Martin," he added.

While he is waiting to be rescued, Neilsen has split his time between writhing in freezing agony and planning sections for his forthcoming book.

"I'm trying to think of chapter headings that sum up the trauma and heroism of my struggle," he said, eating a handful of dirty snow to ward off starvation. "The cover picture will probably be a shot of me looking battered but unbowed as I'm discovered by a search team that's been working day and night to bring me to safety. I'll get the guy who finds me to take my photo.

"Maybe they'll even make a film of my saga, like *Touching the Void*. I'd probably want a less wanky title for it, though."

Although he does not yet represent Neilsen, superagent Harry M. Miller says he is already in advanced negotiations with several energy bar manufacturers for their product to be the one Neilsen is first photographed with after he is found.

Local authorities have called off the search.

Nikolaj shows off his first bit of heroic frostbite

Fears Murdoch takeover will make Wall Street Journal pro-business

Haneef responds to chatroom evidence:

41% of voters wish Howard happy birthday

Australian Government

CITIZENSHIP QUIZ: SAMPLE QUESTIONS

All applicants for Australian citizenship must now answer a series of questions that are either timewastingly obvious, or so obscure that no one born in Australia would know them.

The Australian Government has introduced this quiz to avoid looking like it's preventing non-English speakers from taking citizenship.

Q: How are Members of Parliament chosen?

A: Reluctantly

Q: What are the three levels of government in Australia?

A: Mediocre, Substandard and Local Government

Q: In Australia, it is obligatory to pay tax …

A: Unless your surname is Packer.

Q: As an Australian citizen, I have the right to register my baby born overseas as …

A: An heir to Anna-Nicole Smith

Q: Who is the Queen's representative in Australia?

A: David Flint

Q: How do people become Labor members of parliament?

A: By becoming President of the ACTU

Becoming an Australian Citizen – 2007

Australian Government

CITIZENSHIP QUIZ: SAMPLE QUESTIONS

Q: The population of Australia is …

A: Less than the number of British backpackers

Q: After a Federal election, who forms the new government?

A: A guy more or less the same as the last guy

Q: Serving on a jury is a responsibility of Australian citizenship …

A: If you're too stupid to come up with an excuse

Q: Where is the Parliament of the Commonwealth located?

A: In the middle of nowhere

Q: As an Australian citizen, I have the right to ….

A: Declare things Un-Australian

Q: The first line of the Australian national anthem is …

A: Before kickoff

Q: In Australia, everyone is welcome to practise their religion of choice …

A: As long as it's not Islam

Q: Who do Members of Parliament represent?

A: Macquarie Bank, when they retire

Becoming an Australian Citizen – 2007

Peter Andre happy to have songs illegally downloaded

Peter Andre offers fans the shirt off his back

In the wake of fresh crackdowns on unlawful file-sharing, Peter Andre has announced that he personally has no problem with people making digital copies of his work and trading them online. "If the people want to hear my work, who am I to stand in their way?" he said. "I sang 'Gimme Little Sign' for the fans, not for the money."

The 34-year-old singer/ songwriter, who currently resides in England, has lashed out at greedy record executives for trying to deny potential fans easy access to his back catalogue. "What these studio fatcats don't realise is that it's all about brand extension," said the ARIA award-winner. "Prohibited downloads often lead to increased album purchases. Maybe they should be thinking less about legal action and more about that *Funky Junky: The Best of Peter* idea I pitched them last month."

Andre re-entered the public consciousness courtesy of his glamour model wife Katie "Jordan" Price, who he met on B-grade reality TV show *I'm a Celebrity...Get Me Out Of Here!* in 2004. The pair subsequently recorded a duet of 'A Whole New World', ironic downloads of which first alerted Andre to the potential of viral marketing.

Following the launch of British series *Katie & Peter: The Next Chapter*, Andre has been quietly optimistic about making a musical comeback: "Programs like *Family Guy* and *Futurama* have been renewed years after their cancellation, thanks to a groundswell of grassroots support on the internet. Maybe the same thing can happen for me.

"Check out the comments on YouTube. Someone said the 'Mysterious Girl' filmclip is 'still da best!!!'. You can't buy that kind of publicity – not while Molly Meldrum's refusing to return my calls."

Actual world not as good as World of Warcraft

According to millions of overweight, socially awkward players worldwide, life on Earth cannot hope to compete with a virtual existence comprising heroic adventure, powerful magic and sexy maidens in need of rescue from dragons. For many, attaining level 70 in World of Warcraft is a far more worthy achievement than anything they could hope to accomplish outside the game.

This opinion is not limited to those working in the IT industry. New research has shown that, given the choice between the life of "Dalkyr – gryphon-riding demon slayer" and "Daryl – bus-riding accountant", most people would choose the former, especially when informed that Dalkyr has rippling muscles, flowing golden hair and a "totally sweet Dazzling Longsword".

"It's not surprising that people are turning away from an existence filled with war, famine and disease," said leading psychiatrist Dr Harvey Knowles. "In the realm of Azeroth, death is temporary and the only plague you need to worry about is one that turns you into a ravening undead creature. Even then, you become immune to sleep spells and gain the ability to hold your breath underwater for ages."

Avid player David Canesh, whose real-life relationship with fellow economics student Amy Cavanagh disintegrated during an argument over how much time he was devoting to the killing of imaginary orcs, claims to be happier with his new girlfriend. "Magessa is a smoking hot Night Elf who blows me kisses, LOLs at my jokes and doesn't whinge if I spend all night in the Scarlet Monastery instead of studying," he explained. "What we have is special. It don't care if she is controlled by a middle-aged, bearded guy in Canada."

An area of Azeroth more beautiful than anything Earth can come up with

Things have only escalated with the release of the Burning Crusade add-on, which allows players to gain powerful abilities and enchanted armour sets that make their bill-paying, 9-to-5 existence seem even more mundane.

"I'm concerned about the upcoming Wrath of the Lich King expansion," said Dr Knowles. "If it's as awesome as the video preview promises, I don't know how I'll be able to go on living in the real world."

Freemasons take up rotating EU shadow presidency

World's Greatest Dad now Over the Hill

Ice, meth, crystal, shabu – all these and more are synonyms for methamphetamine (with the exception of 'more'). Ice often seems to be in the headlines these days, usually attached to a bad pun. But is the drug really as bad as the media would have us believe?

Some ice users themselves say other problems are more pressing; like eradicating the thousands of tiny, skin-hugging spiders that won't let them sleep. However commentators continue to warn that the problem is real, and that the media only seems hysterical and paranoid because so many journalists are using ice.

MANUFACTURE

Ice is made in "kitchens" by illegal chemists, who are often assisted by a *sous chef*. The crucial ingredient is pseudoephedrine, found in legally available products like Codral. This is why ice users are able to 'soldier on' after being capsicum-sprayed by police.

The pseudoephedrine is refined into methamphetamine through a complex chemical process that involves accidentally blowing up part of a caravan park.

DISTRIBUTION

Ice manufacture is chiefly controlled by outlaw motorcycle clubs, with some in-law motorcycle clubs also involved. Bikers often try to avoid police attention by doing good works in the community, and sometimes donate leftover ice to charity.

After it is made, ice is hidden inside statues or white goods, ready for its appearance on Border Security. The drug is smuggled interstate by truck drivers, who often disguise their load with freshly grown produce such as tomatoes or cannabis.

USE

A small quantity of ice is shaved off a "rock" of the substance, either by the user or a professional barber. It can be smoked, snorted, injected, or put into a drink. This last process is known as "cubing" or "chilling", and is popular on hot days. Ice can be smoked with a crack pipe, which makes the user look old and wise, like the wizard Gandalf. Expert smokers can blow "ice rings", which are not only pretty, but are also a good way

to entertain malnourished children when the television has been hocked to buy drugs. Ice is generally used recreationally, although there are a small number of professional users.

EFFECTS

Ice causes anxiety, irritability, paranoia, rapid tooth decay, aggression and psychosis, and can also have unpleasant side effects. Users develop delusional beliefs, for example that they want to dance to Italian hi-NRG techno; or that they need a dollar for the train when they have no intention of taking one. They may feel strange urges or compulsions, like the desire to repeatedly perform housework or steal other people's DVD players. Ice can dramatically reduce sexual inhibition to the point where users will consider sleeping with ice addicts.

Ice is habit-forming, with users describing the high as "moreish". Studies show that youth in low income or rural areas are particularly at risk of become addicted, especially in regions without illegal drag racing or gang rapes to keep them occupied.

Ice users may also suffer from social stigma, except if they play professional AFL, in which case they will be lauded for their courage.

CONTROVERSY

Ice has claimed several high profile victims: including Grinspoon singer Phil Jamieson, footballer Ben Cousins and media personality Tim Brunero. Sydney financier Brendan Francis McMahon was charged with bestiality after he allegedly fatally sexually assaulted fifteen rabbits and a guinea pig under the influence of ice (the guinea pig went first). McMahon's initial defense was that the rabbits had consented. When this was rejected, he claimed he had only sexually assaulted one rabbit, and that the other animals were lemmings.

Vanilla Ice has reiterated that he is not affiliated with the drug, but is grateful for the Google hits.

WHERE CAN I GET IT?

Look, you didn't hear it from us, but there's a guy at the pub. He can hook you up with all kinds of freaky shit, man. Shit that'll turn your hair white.

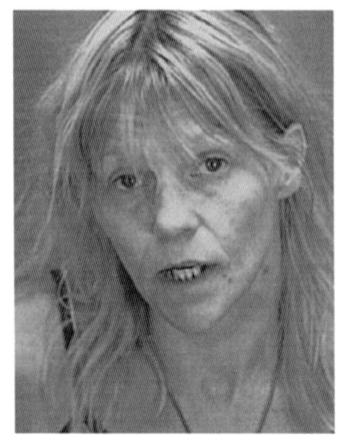

Before and after ice addiction... among its many benefits, the drug can make the user look considerably less dull

Harry Potter series ends: children stop reading

An unprecedented era of book-enjoyment has come to a halt this month, as children around the world finish the final chapter of *Harry Potter and the Deathly Hallows*. "I didn't know whether Harry or Voldemort was going to die in book seven," one fan said. "But I've always known that when the series ended, I'd be saying 'avada kedavra' to my interest in books.

"I'll miss reading, and I wish I could find another lengthy series involving epic magical battles between good and evil, or more rollicking stories set in old-fashioned English public schools," said another teenager. "I've certainly never heard of any, so I guess Rowling's work must be unique."

"When students started picking up *Harry Potter and the Philosopher's Stone*, we were delighted," said school librarian Jenny Lightbody. "But now it looks like I'll have to go back to forcing kids to borrow *Playing Beatie Bow* or *Charlotte's Web* even if they do just leave them in their library bags all week before returning them."

Unfortunately for experts hoping she can rekindle children's love affair with the written word, J.K. Rowling has retired from writing novels to focus on creating a mass market hodge-podge of derivative ideas dressed up

An unidentified teacher forces his pupils to enjoy some light reading

as an original concept.

Warner Bros has told children who may be missing the Potter books to instead catch up with their pals Harry™, Ron™ and Hermione™ at Hogwarts™ in the new World of Wizardry™ at Universal Resort. The new theme park aims to capture the ambience of a centuries-old English castle in a convenient Florida location.

"The park will capture all the magic and wonder of J.K. Rowling's books," a company spokesperson said. "Without the inconvenience of actually reading them."

Children are planning to return to their more traditional pursuits of watching television, playing videogames and juvenile delinquency.

Melbourne underworld leaders to bury the hatchet in each other

Baby now most of Nicole Richie's body weight

APEC: the headlines

Bush to take APEC public holiday off

Putin plans to go without APEC shirt

APEC: Govt builds rabble-proof fence

Rudd hopes he can remember meeting thIs American Bush

Adelaide's new pandas plan to move to Melbourne when they're 18

Protesters unsure whether to make no impact on climate change or free trade

Howard asks Rudd the Chinese word for 'show-off'

Meet the Nominees, part 1: Democrats

The race is on, ladies and gentlemen, for the Democratic Party nomination for President in 2008. In the interests of presenting a fair and balanced view of the upcoming presidential election, we're pleased to bring you the first (and possibly the last, but hell… we can hope, right?) instalment of our Election 2008 (But Really the Vote's in 2007, so Sshhhh) coverage.

Senator Joe Biden

First cab off the rank is Senator Joseph Biden, whose main claim to fame is one of the stupidest, girliest middle names in US political history – "Robinette". (Seriously… what is it with American politicians and their stupid names. Newt? Robinette? BOB DOLE?)

Biden has the distinct advantage of having one of those 'made for daytime TV careers' – you know, tinged with personal tragedy and heartbreak. His first wife and one of his kids died just before he first got elected to the Senate. He also possesses a Sitcom-Father-Unnaturally-White-Smile, a must-have accessory for any candidate.

Biden is the co-author of the 'appease everyone at all costs' third-way approach to 'fixing Iraq'. He's yet to comprehend that it won't work.

His candidacy is hampered by a few key points. First, no one knows who he is. Secondly, he's from Delaware, which means he probably grew up next door to Roseanne. Third, he's a lawyer – three strikes, and you are out, sir! Thanks for playing.

Senator Chris Dodd

Next up is Senator Christopher John Dodd. He's a Gemini, who enjoys long walks on the beach at sunset, playing racquetball with his buddies and making a mockery of his own religious views. A hardcore Roman Catholic, Dodd's onto his second wife already – a sure sign that his faith, a big selling point in any US politician, is shaky at best.

Americans for Democratic Action have Dodd rated at about 95 percent, meaning he's 'left of centre' – interesting for a man who announced his candidacy on the program of disgraced shock jock Don Imus.

Dodd's voting record shows that he's pretty green – he voted along the recommended lines of the League of Conservation Voters 80-100% of the time from 1999 to 2006, and the Justice League of America 75% of the time this year alone. Dodd doesn't like guns, thinks gay civil unions should be allowed, thinks that the embargo on Cuba should be lifted and that the US was too harsh on the Sandinistas. In short, he has 0% chance of success.

Former Senator John Edwards

Former Senator John Edwards is well-known to the American voting public, having come second in the previous race for Vice President and hosted his own TV show where he talks to dead people (Sorry. Wrong guy. That's John Edward. My bad.).

Edwards is a perennial loser, whose career and personal life has been dogged by bad luck and misfortune. His wife has cancer, his son is dead and he's still just a Senator – from North Carolina of all places. Eewww.

Edwards holds the title of Most Hawkish Democrat Candidate™, having co-sponsored Joe "The Mad Bomber" Lieberman's S.J.RES.46 Iraq War Resolution, which knocked the shit out of Iraq, before plunging it into a terrifying civil war that still rages today. He also supported the Patriot Act, which means that he has personally read every single email you've ever sent to the continental United States, and is allowed to lurk on MySpace whenever he likes.

Most notable point in the Edwards campaign came when the website announcing his candidacy went live a day before he did, spilling the beans and ruining any chance he had of making the grand entrance required of a presidential hopeful. He is surrounded by the stench of death and will lose any election he runs for. I know this because I have contacted the spirit world and even they won't vote for him.

Former Senator Mike Gravel

Former Senator Mike Gravel is an interesting character. However, he's hampered from the get-go by a couple of striking points. Firstly, his real name isn't even Mike – it's Maurice. This means that, according to the Steve Miller Band, Gravel isn't even a real person – he's a space cowboy. Also, he's from Springfield, which means he knows the Simpsons. He has only four fingers, but is noted for being 'quite animated'.

Truth be told, Gravel is a bit of a hero. While chairing a do-nothing, go-nowhere Senate sub-committee in 1971 (I think it had something to do with drainage and roads), he entered into the record 4100 pages of a secret Pentagon report on the US involvement in Vietnam, making public the fact that the US had bombed Laos and deliberately expanded its role in the war, despite assurances by then-President Lyndon Johnson that the US wouldn't do much more in Vietnam than buy a few souvenirs and eat a few bowls of pho.

Sadly, Gravel's campaign is doomed to failure. He has no money, and is 50,000 years old (approximately). I'll give you all $10,000 if he wins.

Representative Dennis Kucinich

Oh Dennis, you old fuddy-duddy. Dennis is a loveable old rogue from Cleveland (which means Drew Carey probably voted for him at some stage. Presumably it was while he was still slim enough to fit into a voting booth).

Kucinich is the living, breathing definition of appeaser and apologist, even going so far as to recommend that the United States develop a Cabinet-level Department of Peace. Seriously.

He is, quite possibly, the wettest candidate to ever run for President in the history of the United States. No more death penalty, abortions for everyone, gay people getting married, ratifying the Kyoto Treaty... the list goes on.

Intriguingly, he wants to end the War on Drugs. I urge you all to vote for him now. No one can fight a war on drugs – they're too busy eating donuts and wondering where the remote went this time...

Senator Barack Obama

Arguably the second-most popular black man in America (after Oprah Winfrey), Senator Barack Obama is looking good in the race for the nomination. Pundits believe that his name, as crazy as it is, could either harm or help him, depending on how you look at it. While his surname sounds a bit too much like "Osama" for some people, the fact that his first name means "Where soldiers sleep" should help those who feel that he's soft on terrorism overcome their fears.

Obama's in a strange position on the race issue. Described as "too black" by white voters, and "too white" by black voters, his multi-racial background may hamper his chances a little.

One of Obama's strong points is his admission that he's used drugs. But despite his being a confirmed teenage stoner and coke-head, Obama's had a pretty easy run into politics. He was gifted his Senate seat when strong Republican opponent Jack Ryan was outed by his ex-wife for taking her to sex clubs and asking her to fuck in front of a room full of strangers.

His enormous popularity can be put down to a couple of things, most notably his remarkable physical stature, winsome smile and massive hands. He's a black Anthony Robbins, promising to Awaken the Giant Within America. My money's on him to grab the VP slot and run with Hillary Clinton.

Senator Hillary Rodham Clinton

Hillary's a front runner in this race, and for very good reason. She's got bragging rights over her husband to secure (I was a better President than you could ever hope to be, so get your fat cheating ass back into the kitchen and do some fucking dishes.) And I firmly believe that, with Oprah's help, Hillary will mobilise every single chick in the United States to vote for her. Because the chick vote is solid.

Not short of a dollar, the Delightful Miss Hillary has already raised nearly $30 million to fund her campaign, most of it rumoured to come from the sale of stolen art from the White House and several dodgy land deals in Arkansas. A noted hater of country music, Ms Clinton outraged millions of hat-wearing, gun-toting, line-dancing types by comparing herself to Tammy Wynette. Showing characteristic political aplomb, Clinton fixed the situation by publishing a series of cookie recipes (I wish I was making this up, but I'm not).

With a list of scandals behind her as long as her greedy, money-grubbing arms (all of which end in the suffix "-gate" for reasons no one is able to adequately explain), there's not much room left on her career for any mud to stick. Which means she's gonna win.

Meet the Nominees part 2: Republicans

And so it is with gusto and much fanfare that the band strikes up a stirring rendition of Stars and Stripes Forever, and the Grand Old Party's hopefuls assemble to be measured against the brutal yardstick of truth. Here they are, ladies and gentlemen – the men who would be President, should America decide for some unfathomable reason that the Republicans deserve another chance.

Senator Sam Brownback

Aside from having a name that just sounds dirty (no matter how you say it), Brownback has barely blipped on the radar at all. Mainstream press outlets suggest that he's little-known beyond the borders of his home state, Kansas (home to Dorothy, from the Wizard of Oz… hmmm…) he's using a network of Christian Activists to boost his campaign. So – his name's Brownback, he's a friend of Dorothy and he's relying on Christian Activists to gain notoriety. I think he might be gay.

Not that there's anything wrong with that, of course – unless you're Sam Brownback. He's vehemently opposed to same-sex marriage, and wants intelligent design taught in schools. As a strong Roman Catholic, he's made light of the plight of the Jewish people during WWII by comparing their suffering to that of aborted babies, calling the number of terminations in the United States as 'a holocaust'. He should know by now that the word 'holocaust' has been trademarked by the American Council of Jewry, and that he's leaving himself open to lawsuits aplenty and ridicule at the hands of the "Jewish-Controlled-Media" should he be elected. But it's okay, because he won't be.

John Cox

John Cox, whose main claim to fame is that he's a Certified Practicing Accountant (as opposed to an accountant who has stopped practicing, and is now accounting for real), is a definite man of mystery and numbers. So he probably knows how to access the hidden Tetris game in Microsoft Excel, but probably wouldn't be the kind of person to actually play it.

According to his bio, he has run for the Senate, Congress and even a local government position, failing miserably at every turn. Like any good accountant, his paperwork is right up to date, even if it makes him look like an idiot. So far in 2007, Cox has raised a measly total of $2668 for his campaign. Oh, and loaned himself $745,000 – a very smart move considering he's probably charging himself a 20 point vig. He advocates a GST-style national tax over income tax.

If Cox gets up, I will eat the entire planet. Including bicycles.

Former Governor Jim Gilmore

The American public should be very wary of this bloke. A former spook who served for three years in West Germany, he became the Governor of Virginia. That's where the Pentagon is. So it stands to reason that the man's a spy. But whose side is he on now? He worked counter-intelligence, and I've watched *The Bourne Identity* a couple of times and some James Bond films and I can't figure this guy out at all. He's that good.

Jim Gilmore (if that's even his real name) is a real Republican's Republican. His dedication to tax relief knows no bounds – even when the economy of Virginia was failing after the airport was shut for months due to the 9/11 attacks on the Pentagon, Gilmore pushed ahead with his 'abolish the Virginia Car Tax' agenda. Yes, he kept his promise – but he also crippled the state.

The one positive point: Gilmore's wife has the best middle name in politics – Gatling, after the massive guns on the front of attack helicopters. That should earn him a vote or two.

Former Mayor Rudolph Giuliani

The man who held New York together in the wake of 9/11 is a man on a mission. Consistently calling the Democrats on their inability to handle terrorism, he seems to have forgotten that he himself is very good at handling terrorism after it's happened – no guarantees on how he'll go before it happens though.

That aside, Giuliani's a mess of contradictions – a devoted pro-choice Roman Catholic who's just backed out of his third marriage. Also, when he smiles, it looks like he's got too many top teeth, and no bottom teeth at all. And he's bald.

He'll be the first Italian-American in the White House if he wins, making him the official *capo di tutti capo* for life. Osama Bin Laden can expect to wake up one morning with a yak's head in his bed.

Expect to see Giuliani on the ticket when the nomination dust settles, but where he'll sit is anyone's guess at the moment – I think he's looking good for VP.

Former Governor Mike Huckabee

Hailing from Arkansas, Michael Dale Huckabee is a bit of a dark horse. Following a career in the gubernatorial mansion once inhabited by the Clinton clan, the most striking thing Huckabee's done is lose a massive amount of weight in a very, very short time. Which makes him the Biggest Loser. This included him losing the Governor's position to Mike Beebe.

A shrewd political operator, Huckabee and his missus attempted to circumvent the laws concerning political gifts to incumbent governors by setting up "bridal" registries at a couple of shops prior to a housewarming party they were holding, so that their friends could buy them stuff without them having to report it – the only gifts worth more than $100 allowable to governers are wedding gifts. Of course, he got busted.

He's also under loose investigation over his love of flying – and his loathing of paying for it. The state police jet (they have their own jet??? Awesome… just like Wonder Woman!) has been used by the governor to attend all sorts of official functions, like running in a marathon. Wait… what?

Like most people that have emerged from the Arkansas Governor's mansion, he smells just that little bit bent. Clinton was bent, and Huckabee only went into the job when his predecessor went to the wall over the Whitewater Scandal.

Everything in Arkansas politics is poisonous, this guy included.

Representative Duncan Hunter

I'd love to have a beer with Duncan – but he's a Baptist, so he probably doesn't drink. But by golly, I bet I could go hunting with him. For ducks… or Iraqis. You see, Duncan Hunter is what you'd call a warpig.

He served in Vietnam – I WANNA BE AN AIRBORNE RANGER – and is still a strong advocate of military might, the sword clearly being one helluva lot mightier than the sword. Even his Political Action Committee is a fair indication of where his allegiances lie: "Peace through Strength" it's called, harking back to a military doctrine so out-dated that even Ronald Reagan is spinning in his grave at the thought of it being reworked in the new millennium.

Essentially, it'll mean a return to Cold War era arms races and sabre rattling should Hunter find his way to the White House. My guess is it'll be with China, rather than Russia, as Hunter's an outspoken critic of China in all its forms – trade, race, freedoms, etc. Probably because he fought in Vietnam, and has a longer memory than most other Americans.

Senator John McCain

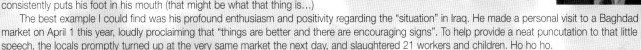

War Hero. Outspoken political critic. Military strongman! John McCain is probably gonna grab the nomination and run with it, despite his supporters, minders, speech-writers and handlers glossing over what is quite possibly the single greatest selling point for voters – he comes as a two-for-one. For President, we have John McCain – and for Vice President, we have that thing growing out of the side of his face. Seriously – what is that? He seems to be able to inflate it at will.

On the plus side is the fact that McCain spent five and a half years as a POW. Not even I will make a joke about that.

I will, however, mention that he likes to make fun of Ugly Little Chelsea Clinton, call Vietnamese people "Gooks" and consistently puts his foot in his mouth (that might be what that thing is…)

The best example I could find was his profound enthusiasm and positivity regarding the "situation" in Iraq. He made a personal visit to a Baghdad market on April 1 this year, loudly proclaiming that "things are better and there are encouraging signs". To help provide a neat puncutation to that little speech, the locals promptly turned up at the very same market the next day, and slaughtered 21 workers and children. Ho ho ho.

And after making a joke about bringing Jon Stewart a souvenir IED from Iraq, he responded to his critics by telling them to lighten up and get a life. Because the War in Iraq is the Funniest Show on TV. McCain will be the Republican nominee, unless things change, in which case he won't be.

Former Governor Mitt Romney

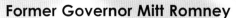

Now this guy's got some serious religious credentials – he's descended from an actual apostle of the Church of Jesus Christ and the Latter Day Saints. No, really… he is. His great-great-grandad Parley Pratt knew Joseph Smith personally, and believed him when he started rambling about an angel called Moroni and a set of golden plates covered in a language that only Smith was able to decipher that Smith 'translated' into the Book of Morman before the angel Moroni took the plates back although some people believe that the plates are buried on the Smith family farm, along with the Sword of Laban that was used by a really, really old Jewish guy to kill a few other people to stop them from taking a set of engraved plates (brass ones this time) that had a copy of his family tree on them, plus yet another set of plates (again brass, this time bell-shaped) that describes something called "The Descent of Ham through the loins of the Pharoah", which sounds not only improbable but incredibly painful.

Romney's great-great-grandad also bought into the whole polygamy thing (greedy sods) and believed that Smith had personally spoken to an angel, and wasn't a lunatic. Romney's great-great-grandad was brutally murdered – which is hardly surprising, given the size of his moustache, and the fact that he took as his second wife a woman who was, inconveniently, already married to someone else.

So – there, in a nutshell, are the religious and family ties that Mitt Romney has to Mormonism. And he wants to be the President. Yeah, right…

Representative Tom Tancredo

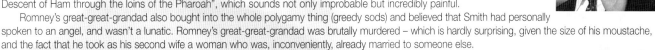

Tom Tancredo, or 'Uncle Tom' as some folks call him (mostly his nephews and nieces, I believe…) is a refreshing breath of stale paleoconservative wind through the burgeoning neo-con ranks of the current administration. He's your typical, old-school conservative – doesn't like immigrants, is anti-abortion and hasn't grasped the irony of calling his Political Action Committee "Team America".

In 2002, Tancredo sponsored the Sudan Peace Act, which stated that "a viable, comprehensive, and internationally sponsored peace process, protected from manipulation, presents the best chance for a permanent resolution of the war, protection of human rights, and a self-sustaining Sudan."

Since then, Sudan has been steadily embroiled in a horrifying civil war, with a death toll somewhere up in the millions, and the US – including Tancredo – has done precisely fucking nothing about it, culminating in the Darfur genocide.

Most recently, Tancredo was banned from appearing at a restaurant called the Rusty Pelican in Miami, after he referred to the city as a Third World Country, in reference to its Hispanic population. Heh… Rusty Pelican. Idiots.

Tommy Thompson

Tommy Thompson was a member of the Bush Cabinet, serving as the Secretary of Health and Human Services. During that time, he championed a number of broad changes to the American healthcare system that benefited medical companies, lawyers and high-level consultancy companies. At the time, he was president of a medical company, a senior partner at a law firm and a senior advisor at a consulting firm. Coincidence? I think not…

He formed a lasting impression with Jewish voters by referring to the Anti-Defamation League as the "Jewish Defence League". Oops.

He's currently on the board of directors of Applied Digital Solutions, the company that makes Veri-Chips – devices designed to be implanted under the skin, which will hold medical and banking records. In other words, he wants to barcode every single person in the United States. This guy's not funny – he's scary. Really scary. FEAR HIM.

Howard 'like Bradman': will fail in last innings

Workplace Relations Minister Joe Hockey called John Howard the "Don Bradman of Australian politics" this week because his magnificent record of victories will be forever tarnished by an embarrassing defeat in his final contest. "I was originally trying to pay tribute to the PM's resilience by evoking the image of the Don batting on and on forever, immovably," Hockey said. "But as a Costello supporter, the other implication doesn't exactly bother me."

Howard has announced he will retire during the next term if he wins, effectively anointing Peter Costello as Leader, in this case of the Opposition. "I have every confidence that when I retire, Peter will do a magnificent job," he said. "He will lead the Liberal Party with great ability and integrity until it dumps him for someone electable."

But Howard has rubbished the now widespread suggestion that he should have retired last year. "I have often said that I would stay for as long as my party wanted me to," he said. "And I've proved again this week that there is no better way of getting the Liberal Party to demand I stay on than floating the prospect of a handover to Costello."

Given the polls, the Prime Minister is now pinning his hopes on a gaffe from Kevin Rudd. But most insiders view the chances of an embarrassing mistake that humiliates him on national television as unlikely. After receiving a boost from his speech to Chinese leader Hu Jintao, the Opposition Leader is determined to deliver every public statement until the election in Mandarin.

Despite his insistence that Howard is Australian politics' Bradmanesque figure, Hockey has privately admitted that Rudd's chance of winning the election is now a record 99.94%.

Howard also emulates Bradman's attitude to foreigners

Zombie enraged by Facebook misrepresentation

Former signwriter and current member of the walking dead, Trevor Fleck, has voiced his outrage at what he calls "the blatant inaccuracies of Facebook's 'Zombies' application". Fleck has called upon his fellow zombies to join him in a Million Mob March against "lame, bullshit online media portrayal of flesh-eating monsters".

"I'd like to see these so-called 'online networkers' deal with a real zombie," moaned Fleck, chewing on a frontal lobe. "You can't just click the 'Ignore' button when an inhumanly strong, insatiably hungry reanimated corpse is bearing down on you, burning with undead hatred and with no desire other than to feast on your dismembered carcass."

Even worse, claims Fleck, are the differing power levels available to Facebook zombies. "Anyone with a rudimentary knowledge of zombie lore would know we're mindless creatures incapable of learning new skills or becoming stronger. It's factually incorrect – and potentially harmful – to give the impression that spreading the zombie infection makes you stronger.

"And I should clarify, no zombie can become a ninja unless they were already one in life."

Max Brooks, author of *The Zombie Survival Guide*, has defended the application. "Certainly, these zombies bear little similarity to their real-world counterparts," he said. "But Trevor should be happy people are raising awareness of zombism. Look at the PR boost vampires got from Anne Rice's novels and Angel."

In related news, the Dead Sheep Alliance is considering launching a class action suit over the SuperPoke! application, which they claim "makes us look like a bunch of tossers".

Trevor cries out for justice, brains

Andrew Johns soils Rugby League's untarnished image

Rugby League fans were shocked this week, by the unbelievable revelation that an overpaid, understimulated sportsman with plenty of free time had experimented with drugs. "I can't believe it," said Newcastle Knights fan Bill Adams. "Who would've thought a footballer would be anything but a moral paragon?"

Andrew 'Joey' Johns, who was caught with ecstasy at a London train station, claimed a stranger had slipped the drug into his pocket at a nightclub: "People are always giving me things without me knowing. Booze, pills, Dally M medals – you name it. I'm usually too out of it to notice."

During a televised interview with Phil Gould, Johns told of his 12-year dalliance with drugs and alcohol. "In some ways, ecstasy actually improved my game," he said. "I'd just get out there and want to tackle every player on the other team and give them a big kiss. The scrums were the best bit, though. They're like a massive group hug."

The Footy Show has handled the issue tastefully, with host Paul Vautin declaring a month-long moratorium on "That's Gold!" calls to mourn the loss of League's innocence. Paul Harrogan has been wearing a black armband, and Reg Reagan has been sporting a 'Bring Back The Spliff' T-shirt.

In the wake of Johns' confession, other prominent Australian sportspeople have admitted to using illicit substances. "I've been taking hallucinogenics for decades," said legendary swimming coach Laurie Lawrence. "I'm amazed no one noticed my erratic behaviour."

Although some of his sponsors have terminated his endorsement contracts, Johns has received messages of support from Kate

This Knight wouldn't mind chasing the dragon

Moss, George Michael and Malcolm Fraser. "This sort of thing can happen to anyone," claimed Wendell Sailor. "Andrew should be thanking his stars they didn't catch him a week earlier, when we were snorting coke off that hooker's tits."

Rock Eisteddfod vows to fight Bishop censorship with dance routine

Schools all across Australia have stridently denied the Federal Government's allegation that left-wing teachers are indoctrinating Rock Eisteddfod participants. "There's only one way to fight the insulting assertion that we don't have minds of our own," said Year 11 student Karen Carlon. "And that's with some snappy choreography to Queen and David Bowie's 'Under Pressure'."

The conflict began when Federal Education Minister Julie Bishop took exception to Davidson High School's entry into the national competition. "This piece, 'Bad Night II', is not only critical of George Bush and the war in Iraq," she said. "It's also completely derivative and creatively uninspired – just a stale rehash of the school's acclaimed

'Bad Night In Baghdad' entry from 2004."

Former Education Minister Brendan Nelson continued the government's attack: "It's immediately obvious to me that the staff is behind this production. No teenager would have enough sense to develop a clear and consistent opinion on global issues. One look at the Young Liberals proves that much."

The students involved have struck back with a large mural depicting Bishop with a Hitler moustache, lycra costumes covered with swastikas and an elaborate dance routine involving stylised goose-stepping and sieg heiling. "There's a big finale where one of our Year 9 students comes out in a gag and straitjacket, with 'free speech' written across his forehead," explained

Students dress in costumes representing the hatred that burns within George Bush's heart

Carlon. "As the opening chords to 'Eye of the Tiger' play, the other students swirl around him, metaphorically beating and burying him."

"Just like the Howard government wants to bury student involvement in politics," interjected drama

teacher Georgina Adams. "And suppress fair pay and conditions for teachers."

The Howard Government has vowed to continue fighting against the scourge of left-wing indoctrination by yet again increasing its funding for private schools.

Son finds dad's porn collection 'disappointing'

He thought he had hit the mother lode, but 14-year-old Reggie Molina has expressed dismay at the paltry state of his father's pornography collection. "Dad usually goes up to the shed and locks the door when he gets home from work," Reggie explained. "I knew there'd be something hidden away in there that I'd be interested in." Instead of the hard-core barely legal filth he is used to seeing on the internet and DVDs belonging to his older cousins, the only things Reggie found in his father's poorly hidden workbag were some faded

copies of *People* magazine and a battered June 1989 edition of *Girls of Penthouse*. None were able to arouse the youngster's jaded interest.

"I suppose it's normal for someone of Dad's age to have those kind of urges," he said. "Natural curiosity. I just thought he might have outgrown that sort of thing a long time ago, like I did when I was nine. I feel a bit embarrassed for him. I mean – that stuff is so tame. Plus, all the women had hair on their vaginas, which looked really weird. It must've been some kind of fetish in the

early 90s."

Molina flicked through the dated pictorials in search of cum shots, but was able to find none. "I can understand not having a double penetration, but not even a single? Where did he get these things – a pre-school?"

"I haven't even seen a model get bukkaked yet," complained Reggie. "How can anyone be expected to get aroused by a naked lady just standing there with a smile on her face?"

Experts predict Molina will also find his first sexual experience disappointing, since

A disappointing porno

it is unlikely to involve any kind of anal rampage, or a muscly black man he can high-five over a woman's back.

Iraq wins Asian Cup: celebratory gunfire to continue indefinitely

Iraq's football team has won its first ever major trophy after defeating Saudi Arabia in the finals of this year's Asian Football Cup, and ecstatic Baghdad residents diverted their regular gunfire into the air in celebration.

"This win has unified Iraq," said one Sunni insurgent as he discharged his pistol into the air. "The only thing that could make this day any better is if my joyful bullet ended up in a Shiite."

Every win during the team's progression to the finals was marred by numerous deaths on the streets of Baghdad, mystifying the occupying American troops. "So it's OK for them to spray around bullets whenever something good happens, but when we Americans try to bring really good news, like the removal of Saddam Hussein, they can't stomach a little bit of aerial bombardment," one marine said. "I'll never understand this place."

The side credits its remarkable triumph on the field to being more motivated than the other teams in the competition. "Of course, we wanted to achieve something that would bring joy to our troubled land," team captain Younis Mahmoud said. "But we were mainly motivated by knowing that as soon as we were eliminated, we'd have to go back home."

Despite the victory being portrayed as a win against the odds, coach Jorvan Vieira said he was confident his team could prevail in difficult conditions. "No team has more experience with shootouts," he said.

After his phenomenal success winning a prestigious trophy with a hastily cobbled-together team, Vieira has been tapped to take on an even tougher assignment: achieving a credible World Cup performance from England.

Iraqis celebrating, or conducting an insurgency, or both

The victorious team's return to Baghdad is expected to be the first event in the city's recent history where anyone has actually been welcomed with garlands of flowers.

Fears Murdoch takeover will make Wall Street Journal pro-business

Costello better Treasurer, Howard better at doing numbers

Packer invests more in gambling: marries again

After building casinos in Macau and Hong Kong, James Packer has increased his exposure to the gambling industry after deciding to chance his fortune on another wife. Most experts rate the mogul's business decisions as considerably more sound than those he makes about his personal life. "The Asian gambling market will be around for the long haul," one analyst said. "Whereas historical performance figures show that James' model acquisitions leave him significantly in the red after a few years."

But many of the groom's friends have applauded Packer's choice of Erica Baxter. "James knows that this girl isn't quite so likely to tire of him, since she was able to spend all those years with Jason Donovan," a Packer associate revealed. "Erica's just happy to have a partner who's perceived as heterosexual."

In an attempt to protect his fortune, Packer has insisted on a prenuptial agreement, and so has new wife Erica Baxter, who has specified that in the event of their divorce, her husband must retain custody of the Church of Scientology.

Close Packer buddy Tom Cruise attended the ceremony in the South of France, but did not perform a Scientology wedding ceremony, as had been rumoured. "He was going to marry them, but there were concerns about the sermon," an inside source disclosed. "Erica felt that 'The Evils of Psychiatry' wasn't an appropriate topic."

Packer's first wife, Jodhi Meares, said she hoped the newlyweds would live happily ever after. "And I can tell you Erica will, if she ever cashes in her divorce settlement," she said.

Despite the doubts over his marital prospects, many in the business world have applauded Packer's decision to focus exclusively on casinos. "James is pleased to be getting out of Channel Nine," a PBL insider said. "and into the entertainment business."

Once he tires of her, Packer hopes to offload Baxter to an unsuspecting private equity outfit

Share market goes from subprime to ridiculous

Matthew Reilly book correctly judged by cover

Pauline reinvents herself: now hates Muslims

Libs complain new ACTU leader is beholden to unions

New ACTU leader Jeff Lawrence has come under heavy fire from the Coalition, who claim he is little more than a puppet of the union movement. "The ACTU can't even pretend it's free from the influence of the union movement," said Health Minister Tony Abbott in a parliamentary broadside. "And here they are, nominating another faceless union bureaucrat to be their leader. The last ACTU leader was a union man, this bloke's a union man, and mark my words – the next bloke will be a union man too," said Abbott, to loud calls of 'hear hear' from the the Government benches.

Abbott found a surprise ally in former Prime Minister Paul Keating, who said the ACTU needed to remain independent of the union movement if it wanted to remain relevant. He went on to blame the Labor Party, his former advisors, Julia Gillard, John Howard, Mark Latham, and Greg Combet for the current state of affairs, while also singling out everyone else but himself for more criticism.

Lawrence denies being a passionate supporter of trade unionism. The incoming ACTU Secretary says he will follow in the footsteps of his predecessors by simply marking time until he's parachuted into a safe seat.

Kevin Rudd welcomed the appointment, and wished Lawrence well. "I hope he acts as a passionate advocate for his organisation," he said. "Unless he's too passionate, in which case we'll expel him from the Labor Party."

"Someday, I could be Prime Minister, like Bob Hawke," said Lawrence. "Then I'll really be able to prove I'm not beholden to the unions."

Lawrence...puppet master of the ACTU

The Blair Years

Tony Blair – for many, he symbolised the British prime ministership for a number of years. Ushering in years of Tony rule after years of Tory rule, the legacy he left behind was a mixed one. He banned fox hunting, but legalised the hunting of Brazilian civilians. He championed the poor, while the poor Championed their wardrobes. He will be remembered for starting the War in Iraq, and finishing the credibility of the British Commonwealth. He was the people's Princess, and here, we capture his tenure in the manner he would wish – in sound bites.

Blair's views on marijuana decriminalisation were formed early.

Blair legalised civil partnerships, but ultimately declined Schwarzenegger's proposal.

Blair often defeated weaker opponent with relish. Here, he thrashed Tim Henman in straight sets, ending the journeyman's Wimbledon dreams for another year.

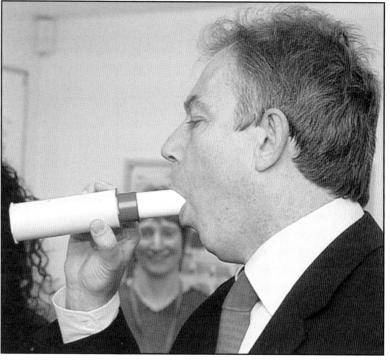

Towards the end, even his own party agreed that Blair totally blew.

Blair and Bush developed a close bond, but some worried that Blair would fall for the inevitable "pull my finger" routine.

Blair responds by requesting that Bush "smell the cheese".

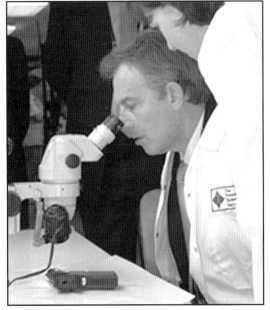

To the end, Blair remained convinced that the WMD would eventually be found in Iraq, and insisted more searching was required.

Blair denied that he kept the British public in the dark on Iraq, but admitted the Iraqi public were kept in the dark. Here he promises to fix their power shortages.

"Please stop trying to explain Iraq. Please stop trying to explain Iraq. Please stop…"

Like the British public, Cherie ultimately found her husband tiresome.

Madonna's African child shocked by Hollywood: 'more starvation than at home'

They had imagined America and England as lands of plenty, where no one wanted for food. But now, the adopted children of high-powered celebrity couples say they are appalled at the deprived circumstances they've found themselves in. Madonna's new son, Malawian David Banda, says his mother lives in a state of almost constant malnutrition.

The allegations will only add to the controversy surrounding the adoption. Malawian groups have accused the star of contravening the country's strict adoption laws, which allow exceptions to the one-year waiting period only for slaves, soldiers and child prostitutes. Banda's father expressed reservations about the decision, saying he didn't know the situation was permanent, and had not seen Madonna act when he signed over his child's rights.

"Madonna is everything I could hope for in a mother," he says. "She even walks around half-naked to make me feel more at home. But she will often go days without eating, and when food does arrive, it's nothing more than a handful of brown rice and a few vegetables," he says. "At first I thought this country must be suffering from a terrible drought or civil war, but she assures me that's not the case."

Diet is not the only cause for concern. According to Banda, many celebrities still practise crude forms of pre-modern medicine, often relying on talismans to ward off disease and misfortune. "Even in Malawi, we've known for generations that cupping – putting hot glass on people to blister the skin – is quackery. But apparently the whole Western medical establishment carries less weight than a recommendation from Gywneth Paltrow."

Banda says he plans to discuss

Madonna & Child: a Like A Virgin birth

the issue with other adoptees at the Oscars early next year, where African children are tipped to be the hottest red-carpet accessories.

Creative anachronist would last five seconds in Middle Ages

Despite his intense affection for the period, history buff and member of the Society for Creative Anachronism, Brendan "Sir Lysander" Hanrahan, would likely be dead within moments of arriving in Merrie Englannd, say experts.

"To be perfectly honest, Brendan could never be a knight," explains History professor Malcolm Faulconbridge. "His common blood aside, I doubt he'd survive his first cup of water from that period, let alone an actual joust. A weak yet overweight child like him would have been very lucky to reach adulthood." Faulconbridge also points out that becoming a knight involved laying on a stone floor for a night, an experience likely to promote an acute asthma attack in Hanrahan.

Should his oft-repeated dream of time travel to that period ever come true, Hanharan's physically unimposing presence would make the self-described "heraldry nut" a sure target for thieves and brigands. The electrical engineering student and part-time lute player could also die in a tourney, as he erroneously believes himself to be "an experienced hand-to-hand fighter".

"I've mastered the broadsword, the halberd, and the mace," says Hanrahan, by which he means different shaped sticks covered in tape.

"Lysander's completely blind without his glasses," said fellow SCA member Julia "Sortiarius Sifaka" Tannen, whom Hanrahan often tries to woo with atonal balladry. "As soon as he lost them, he'd be cactus. I, on the other hand, have perfect 20/20 vision. I'd probably end up a duchess or something."

Experts agree that if Hanrahan did survive his first evening in the Middle Ages, he would most likely find employment as a stablehand, a position with meagre rations, where poor performance would result in beatings. "Brendan believes that he would be better off hundreds of years ago, where his knowledge of falconry and

Creative anachronist: Sir Lysander calls for a wench and another mug of Red Bull

Morris dancing would carry greater social status," said Etheridge. "In fact, he would be even more despised than he is in the 21st century. Although it's a little less likely people would keep calling him a fag."

Howard supports climate change: to 'radioactive'

John Howard has backed nuclear power as a way of combating climate change. "Nuclear power is the way to help reduce greenhouse gas emissions," he said. "And it won't have any impact on our climate, unless you count a little bit of radioactive rain." Howard's claims have been supported by leading nuclear scientists, who stated that while nuclear reactors sometimes emit deadly clouds of highly radioactive caesium, iodine and strontium, they never produce carbon dioxide.

The Prime Minister also pointed out that in some instances, producing nuclear power can even reduce electricity consumption as well. "Look at the town of Chernobyl," he said. "They're still using close to zero electricity."

Howard's claims of environmental benefits were supported by an inquiry he commissioned into nuclear power. The panel, chaired by Ziggy Switkowski, found that nuclear power would benefit those in the cities, and only pose health risks to those in the rural areas where the power stations would be located, a risk

Howard may grow mushroom clouds in his greenhouse

Switkowski dismissed. "As the former CEO of Telstra, I can tell you that there's no need to worry about the bush," he said.

Despite his new-found commitment to climate change, the Prime Minister still refuses to ratify the Kyoto targets. But he pointed out that his plan to introduce nuclear power does raise the possibility of

other Japanese targets, such as Hiroshima and Nagasaki.

Most political commentators have dismissed Howard's attempts to portray himself as passionate about the environment, calling them even more unconvincing than Peter Garrett's attempts to pretend that he isn't.

MC's role 'largely ceremonial'

Tim Ferguson's son to form Larry Anthony All Stars

Mighell gets high wages for union members: Rudd's wife sent in

Reports that Victorian ETU Secretary Dean Mighell once negotiated excellent deals for his members in the construction industry have led to the urgent deployment of Therese Rein. The Opposition Leader's wife will ensure that the workers negotiate away their generous entitlements for only 45c an hour.

Rein said that the millions her company has made from Government contracts should not be taken as an endorsement of the Coalition's workplace policies. "As anyone who's ever worked for one of my companies will tell you, I'm completely against their new fairness test," she said.

"And despite the profits Ingeus has made from the Coalition's reforms, never let it be said that I don't want my husband to become Prime Minister," she added. "If he wins the election, there'll be a raft of extra people looking for work."

The Mighell situation has had far-reaching effects on the ALP. The new leader's insistence that the ALP should no longer welcome under-the-table bullying tactics has led to the resignation of every single sitting MP, incluing Rudd himself.

In response to his sacking, Mighell criticised Kevin Rudd for expelling him from the ALP,

The Rudd family has reduced Mighell's work choices

pointing out that the party is in no position to be turning away members who are actually alive.

The union boss says he is so outraged by his treatment that he won't seek to rejoin Labor until at least the next election, where he will be handed a safe seat as a reward for making Kevin Rudd look tough on unions.

God dismisses gambling-related prayer

God has pointedly ignored a request for divine intervention in a greyhound race. Despite the repeated, fervent pleading of a number of race-goers at the Dapto Dogs, the popular deity allowed 11/1 outsider Indiana Bones to run last. "God knew what I wanted, and He knew how badly I wanted it," said punter Clive Deville. "The fact that Indiana Bones ran last… well, it's shaken my faith in the Judeo-Christian ethos, that's for sure."

The exact wording of Deville's prayer, "Please, God, please let this trifecta happen," left no doubt as to the outcome desired by the petitioner. "Dirtbox Daisy winning would have needed a miracle", said Jehovah. "And I'm not in the business of providing miracles to people

who haven't set foot inside a church since 1993."

Theologians have argued the implications of this event since late last week: "Greyhounds have choice like the rest of us. The Lord has promised He won't interfere with our free will, why is why He will not magically make a dog run faster than it otherwise would. It's all spelled out in Leviticus. Or Galatians. I forget which. It would also be a breach of Greyhound Association rules."

This marks the 37-trillionth selfish prayer the Almighty has ignored since time began. Previous deific refusals have involved Collingwood winning the 2002 or 2003 AFL Grand Final, sex with any member of the Pussycat Dolls and the making of "a

Gambling prayer: the dramatic photo finish, which God failed to take a hand in

new Star Wars movie to settle the question of Princess Leia's Jedi potentiality once and for all".

"I thought I'd made it pretty clear in the Bible that I wasn't a big fan of adultery, but people never seem to stop asking me about it. I'm not going to help people 'bang chicks', no matter how hot

they are." God also stated for the record that He was reluctant to give men erections after a big night of drinking, and that He was not going to smite anyone's boss, unless He was planning to anyway, as part of his "Mysterious Ways" project.

God also noted he is tired of being thanked it's Friday.

James Blundell scores first-ever young fan

After almost two decades of catering to the musical tastes of the middle-aged, country singer James Blundell finally learned the secret of cornering the youth market – have regular sex with them. "I saw Jesse Curran at one of my concerts," he revealed. "At first I thought she must've been there with her dad, but it turned out she was just wanted to hear 'Way Out West' live."

Curran, an *Australian Idol* contestant, claims she loves 43-year-old Blundell for more than just his rugged good looks and jackaroo background. "I've been listening to James' songs ever since he released 'Hand It Down' in 1990," she said. "I remember it well, because my second-class teacher used to play it while we did process writing."

Critics have called Blundell's new relationship a "clever marketing ploy" that is guaranteed to put him in touch with the younger generation. "Publicists are already referring to the couple as JesseJames," said promoter Michael Chugg. "I think the time is right for James to put on an under-18s show.

"Especially now he's shown he's willing to do all-ages."

Meanwhile, Lidia Blundell has hit out at her estranged husband's claims that she was to blame for the break-up: "James came home early one day, and caught me listening to a Shannon Noll album. If he thinks going out with that little bitch is some kind of payback, just wait until I get my hands on Damien Leith's phone number!"

Blundell is reportedly considering an affair with an old-age pensioner, "just to widen my appeal a bit further". Marcia Hines was unavailable for comment.

James: livin' and a-workin' on young women's nubile bodies

Sydney's top 10 APEC sights

While you're in Australia's biggest city for the APEC summit, why not enjoy some sightseeing at some of Sydney's world-famous tourist attractions? This top 10 list has been updated to take account of the special security conditions prevailing during the conference.

1. Sydney Harbour and the Opera House

Sydney's harbour is world famous, and its legendary Opera House is regularly named as one of the most beautiful buildings in the world. Unfortunately, during APEC, you may not visit the building, or approach it, or travel on the harbour, or even look at the harbour because of the security barriers around most of the major waterside vantage points. But postcards are readily available during your stay and, trust us, it's all very beautiful.

2. Taronga Zoo

All of the best animals have been moved to Garden Island for the private enjoyment of world leaders, but Taronga Zoo still boasts some state-of-the-art empty cages.

3. Great Wall of Sydney

Scotland has Hadrian's Wall, China its Great Wall, and now Sydney has a massive wall around much of the city. Our Great Wall may not be visible from space (but then again nor is the Chinese one, despite the urban myth) but it's certainly an eyesore in most of the city. Like the Great Wall of China, you can walk along sections of it. But unlike the Great Wall, if you do so, you will be arrested, or possibly shot.

4. Historic Parramatta

During the conference, NSW Police are running free courtesy buses to this historic centre, located by the picturesque Parramatta River. Under the special APEC legislation, those arrested in the APEC Zone will be transported to Parramatta for charging. Those planning on availing themselves of this convenient service should note that, because of the bars over the windows, views from the buses will be limited. Ditto the cells.

5. Wet 'n' Wild water cannon

Forget the Manly Waterworks. During APEC, water-time fun has come to the heart of the city! A quick blast from the police's high-powered water cannon will have you drenched in moments. Particularly recommended for visiting protesters who haven't washed in months.

6. The Running of the Motorcades

In Pamplona, tourists run down cobbled streets in front of enraged bulls. But in Sydney this week, feral protesters will run in front of presidential motorcades in a pointless attempt to disrupt them. It's likely to be bloodier than any running of the bulls.

7. Little Baghdad

Sydney is known for its many colourful ethnic neighbourhoods, which bring a taste of their home country to create a rich multicultural patchwork. During the meeting, Sydneysiders will have a chance to sample Baghdad's renowned Green Zone via the intense security of the APEC Zone, which will protect those inside from the indignity of any contact with ordinary people in the country they're visiting.

8. Street racing

Sydney's many hoons love speeding around the city's renowned street racing circuits, such as the Hickson Road area. During APEC, a single circuit can take hours thanks to the frequent traffic interruptions! You've never had a race that lasted this long.

9. Bondi Beach

The famous beach is also known for its high concentration of intoxicated tourists, especially on the Sunday of the conference when Janette Howard hosts her counterparts at Bondi Icebergs for an afternoon on the pink champagne.

10. Rifle range

It's one big gun fair for shooting aficionados during APEC, with some of the latest paramilitary equipment being deployed on rooftops around the city. And, during the meeting, Sydney is being converted into the world's largest sniper rifle range. Note that gun enthusiasts should not attempt to purchase any of the weapons on display, or attempt to trade any of their own firearms with those on official duty, lest they themselves are used for target practice.

Five things I learned this year
from the bile duct of Gregor Stronach

1) John Howard has died

As the beige tide of mediocrity that is Kevin Rudd begins his final surge into the Lodge, we are honour-bound to take pause and remember the man in whose wake he has risen. Prime Minister John Howard, fearless leader and ruthless war dog, is finally dying.

Not literally of course (although, it could be argued that we're all marching inexorably to our own grave at any given moment…). But still, the Australian public is hovering by the bedside of John Howard's career, peering myopically over the shoulder of the spin doctors as they prepare to remove the feeding tubes, and let him wither and croak like Terry Schiavo.

(I'm not sure if John Howard has an allergy to nuts, but it might go some way towards explaining that weird rash he gets on his chin. I'm just sayin'…)

Regardless, it is very clearly the end for the Midget of Bennelong. His own seat, which he's held in his tiny, vice-like grip since 1974, is in a perilous state. With only a shade over four percent as a safety margin, a recent redistribution and a stunningly popular Labor candidate waiting in the wings to swoop and steal the mantle, things look grim. Meathook Grim.

So let us be the first to call time of death – the moment when Howard's career jumped the shark, never to return to the days when he had clarity, real power, and hair. Of sorts.

Howard will fall at the next election, and his passing means that the Coalition had better have been stockpiling food and blankets, in preparation for a long and lonely winter in the wilderness. The power vacuum at the head of the Liberal Party is as profound as the one found between Paris Hilton's ears. Who will lead? Who will follow? Who knows? But then, who cares?

2) APEC, and who it killed

The jewel in Sydney's crown for 2007 was the APEC summit – a week-long gabfest that created incredible hype…and little else.

As a proud Sydneysider, I was subjected to the police-state tactics of the government as it sought to avoid any embarrassment, even at the cost of the basic freedoms for which Australia is internationally famous. Military helicopters buzzed my city. Snipers (dressed gaily in day-glo vests, no less) crouched on rooftops, their high-grade weapons at the ready, should something go horribly awry.

The protests were beyond boring. Were

President Bush farewells the Organisation of the Petroleum Exporting Countries

there bongo-playing hippies? Oh yeah, there were. Did they have massive banners full of awful puns? Yep! And were their flyers poorly photocopied? You bet!

But for all their posturing and agitating, nothing happened. The protests were a fizzer. No one gave a shit. For the most part, Sydney was mildly inconvenienced at worst, and given a bit of a sick thrill at best, by the heavy-handed police presence. No – the people of Australia weren't the victims of APEC – the APEC leaders were. Let's take a look at the toll.

Of the 21 world leaders on parade at the event, several are now in the firing line, and won't be leaders within a couple of months. George Bush – gone, as his term as President expires. Vladimir Putin is stepping down. The PM of Japan, Toyota Suzuki or whatever his name is, has resigned. John Howard is about to be voted out of office. And the list goes on, giving credence to my theory that the APEC summit was the political equivalent of having your private parts mauled by a deranged leper in a dark Turkish alleyway.

The only people to do well out of APEC were the cops, who earned themselves a handy amount of overtime pay, and our very own Chaser lads, who went from being mildly famous in Australia to mildly internationally famous.

As for the results of the summit – well, we got a half-arsed commitment from a bunch of retiring and soon-to-be-ousted leaders to do something or other about

John Howard coped surprisingly well with Gregor's announcement of his demise

the wavering spectre of global warming. Meh. They could have saved themselves the bother, stayed home and phoned it in. It would have made gatecrashing a whole lot harder.

3) It's getting hot in here...

2007 will long be remembered as the year of global warming. At least, that's how I'll see it, as I revel in the fact that it rains a whole lot less in Australia, making riding a motorcycle that much more enjoyable.

Honestly – besides Al Gore, could we have cared less about climate change this year? It went from serious social issue to mass-market hysteria, spawning films, books, study tours and – unbelievably – rock concerts. Impossibly massive rock extravaganzas, broadcast around the world.

I was gobsmacked – even worse than usual, too – by the outright lunacy of the Live Earth shows. I mean, seriously – primped and preened rock stars travelling by fossil-fuel burning private jets to the four corners of the globe to sing in massive, environmentally unfriendly concrete stadiums in front of millions of rubbish-tossing, methane-producing punters… The hypocrisy was breathtaking.

I can tell you that it raised the temperature at my place during the event, as I burned countless calories wailing at the TV and throwing furniture. I howled with rage at the uber-smug performers as they carried on about how we can all do our bit, while they burned up unimaginable amounts of electricity singing old, shit songs that no one likes anymore. Yes, I'm talking about you, Sting.

The end result? A clean up bill that rivals the worst rock excesses of the 1970s, Al Gore looking even more pleased with himself and a small army of copycat documentary makers, including the abysmal talents of Leonardo Di Fucking Caprio…

My solution, unfortunately, isn't green enough to work. But I reckon it's worth a shot. I say we get all the global warming enviroweenies, their documentaries, books, pamphlets and ideas, and burn 'em. Torch the whole lot – touch off a blaze that takes 1000 years to extinguish. It won't help the environment any, but it'll make me feel a whole lot better.

4) Pop will undereat itself

Tinsel Town produced a stunning array of tabloid fodder in 2007. The list of who fucked who, nearly overdosed, went to rehab, crashed their car, married someone stupid, divorced someone even dumber or – incredibly – released a record, is as long as my arm. And still growing.

The title of Trashbag of the Year absolutely has to go to Britney Spears, narrowly edging out perennial rehab attendee Lindsay Lohan and Paris Hilton. Not even Owen Wilson's last-minute attempt on his own life was enough to knock Britney off her pedestal.

Ms Spears is a walking testament to the excesses of the American Dream – how one girl can go from Trailer Trash to Really Wealthy Trailer Trash without batting an eyelid. Her rehab antics were awesome – her post-rehab head-shaving and photographer-bashing was even better. The ongoing saga that suggests that Kevin Federline might be a better parent (and really, who amongst us saw that coming?) is simply brilliant.

But the jewel in the crown was Britney's comeback appearance at the MTV awards. The sight of a portly lass in sequined underwear forgetting the lyrics to her own song was priceless. Her lacklustre attempts to cover it up even more so. By the end, she looked like she had Parkinson's disease, and needed a good lie down.

God love you, Britney – you're trashier than a Staten Island garbage barge. Don't ever forget where you came from, though. Actually there's not much chance of that, because god knows you'll be moving back into a home with wheels any day now.

5) People die

It's been a big year for dead people – and the planet has ceased to be called home by a stellar cast of famous folks who have shuffled from this mortal coil (whatever the fuck that means) and gone to heaven, or

The less embarrassing of Britney's two shaved-body parts incidents of 2007

hell, depending on whether they had paid their religious membership dues. Here are the dead people highlights of 2007.

Luciano Pavarotti finally reached maximum density and waddled to the grave. Word on the street is that it took nineteen sopranos and a front end loader to shift his corpse. The three tenors became two tenors, a nice little outcome for Placido Domingo and the other one no one knows – sales of the CDs will soar on the news of Pavarotti's death, and they now only have to split the profits two ways. Nice!

The glamorous world of TV evangelism took two heavy hits this year, after the Rev. Jerry Falwell went to meet his boss, and Tammy Faye Bakker was recalled to the house of Satan. Christians around the world were saddened by the news of the passing of both of these people, but for different reasons – Falwell will be missed by his flock, while Bakker's legion of duped creditors realise that they will never see the money they donated to be spent on bibles for El Salvador ever again.

Closer to home, Australia lost Stan Zemanek, who was taken screaming to his grave. He took his final call-in from the Grim Reaper himself. Outwardly, Australia mourned his passing, with tributes flowing in from all sectors of the media. Privately, we all thought he was a prick. But that's the way it goes…

Andrews now claiming Haneef visited Scores

The beleaguered Immigration Minister, Kevin Andrews, is now claiming that Dr Mohamed Haneef visited a New York strip club in 2003. Andrews says the Australian Federal Police believe that Haneef visited Scores with a shady character known for his dubious morals, but the doctor has strenuously denied knowing Col Allan.

Dr Haneef also pointed out that as a practising Muslim, he was even more unlikely to have been drunk than Kevin Rudd, and that there was no reason anyone would drink with the editor of the *New York Post* otherwise.

But Andrews rejected Haneef's claims, saying that he is party to other evidence linking Haneef to Scores that cannot be made public because it would jeopardise an ongoing investigation. He later backed up his decision by releasing excerpts of Haneef's interrogation which sounded incriminating until they were understood in their proper context.

Andrews later admitted that the AFP's desperate search for evidence that would make his decision seem reasonable was the only ongoing investigation that actually involved Dr Haneef.

Queensland Premier Peter Beattie once again came to Dr Haneef's defence, saying that even if he had visited

Rudd's education policy

Scores, he was glad to hear that, like Rudd, the doctor had "some blood in his veins". Given the state of the Queensland hospital system, Beattie said, that was all that was required for him to be invited to return to work.

Kevin Rudd again refused to disagree with Howard over Haneef, but renewed his calls for a full judicial inquiry into the claims. To assist the process, the Opposition Leader offered to cross-examine the relevant lap-dancers personally.

Khalid Sheikh Mohammed confesses to 9/11, Bali, JonBenet, 'anything to make it stop'

Costello celebrates birthday: everyone guesses his wish

Britney Spears declared Mother of the Year

In a victory bound to take the troubled singer's mind off her custody battle, Britney Spears has been crowned Mother of the Year after a nationwide search. The competition spanned a variety of criteria, including community involvement, life/work balance and erratic behaviour. "No matter how many nominees we looked at, Britney's name came up again and again," said judge Julia Burris. "It's just a shame she was too drunk to come to the awards ceremony.

"Each new revelation from her ex-bodyguards and assistants shows what a balanced person and wonderful mother Britney is," said Burris. "Every child dreams of a parent who takes care to hire an appropriate nanny to look after them while she goes out clubbing with no knickers on."

According to a story leaked exclusively to *NW*, *Famous* and *New Idea*, Spears celebrated her win by stripping naked in front of her housekeeper, taking an unspecified number of drugs and quietly sobbing while devouring a entire suckling pig. "I've never been so happy," she reportedly said, before drink-driving with her sons on her lap.

The announcement has come as a blow to Britney's ex, Kevin Federline, who is attempting to take legal custody of the children. "When I saw Britney's performance at the MTV Video Music Awards, I thought I had this thing in the bag," he said. "Obviously I'd forgotten what an immoral, mooching deadshit I am."

Spears' excellent parenting has sparked waves of jealousy among the local schoolyards. "Jayden and Sean Preston are so lucky," said eight-year-old Tommy Pearson. "Their mummy sings to them, and buys them cool clothes, and shows them what a nervous breakdown looks like close-up."

Britney's own mother, Lynne Bridges, picked up second prize in the contest.

Britney arrives to collect her kids from childcare

President Bush revises Howard nickname to 'Man of Steel Boots'

Melbourne Cup to be raced at Royal Phlegmington

Keith Richards denies snorting father's ashes, admits injecting them

Geriatric rockstar Keith Richards has hit out at the media, claiming he was joking when he told British music mag *NME* he had snorted his dad Bert's remains in 2002. The Rolling Stones guitarist says the media are "making a mountain out of a relatively small pile of cadaver-infused cocaine."

"I had too much respect for my father to bury his ashes in my nostrils," he said. "The collapsing veins in my arm were a far more suitable resting place for the man who brought me into this world. Now he can live forever inside me, next to that amazing smack Janis Joplin gave me in 1969."

No stranger to illegal chemicals, Richards has been arrested several times for drug use, although this is the first time an immediate family member has been involved. In 1967, he was picked up by Sussex police while in possession of a small baggie of grey powder, later traced to a local crematorium, and 10 years later Canadian police busted him with 22 grams of Brian Jones he'd been saving "for a special occasion".

But Richards, who recently took a cameo role in *Pirates of the Caribbean III*, says his reputation has been greatly exaggerated. "How much of a wild man can you be when you appear in a movie based on a Disneyland ride?" he asked. "Though Johnny Depp and I did split half a gram of River Phoenix. That guy was hardcore."

Richards is yet to deny other persistent rumours, including claims he had all his blood replaced to beat drug addiction, once stayed awake for nine days straight and is actually a walking corpse, animated by necromantic magic.

Richards has admitted he still takes a little piece of the Stones' late guitarist with him wherever he goes

Matthew Newton's family feud now outrating Bert's

Gamblers' families welcome equine flu

While the racing world reels from the devastating effects of equine flu, there is one group feeling optimistic about the future. "It's a shame those trainers and horse owners have lost millions of dollars," said gambling addict Tommy Vincent. "But on the plus side, my son can get those braces he needs."

"Die, you four-legged homewreckers," screamed housewife Flo Black, whose husband routinely blows all his family's grocery-shopping money at the track, upon hearing of the viral outbreak. "Cough yourselves to death and rot in your mucus-ridden graves."

According to experts, horse flu has had the biggest impact on Australia's gambling industry since a group of Victorian poker machines caught a computer virus in 2001. "Just like those days, we can look forward to seeing a rise in family boardgame nights and a decrease in drunken arguments and barrel-wearing," said family psychologist Lyn Fields.

Other sectors are feeling the effects of the illness, with Federal Agriculture Minister Peter McGauran offering emergency relief packages to a number of milliners and fascinator designers. "These people are the forgotten victims of equine flu," he said. "Without racing carnivals, there's really no reason for anyone to wear the ridiculous headgear that is their bread and butter."

"It's a terrible shame about the horses – but at least I

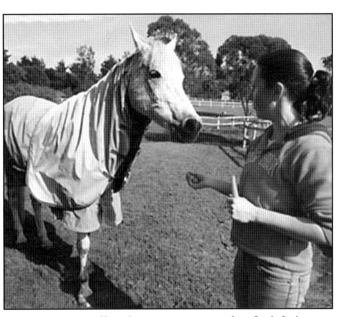

A horse owner offers her nag some equine Sudafed

still have the dishlickers," said lovable punter Jack Bleakley, withdrawing a large sum of money from his wife's savings account. "All I need is one trifecta, and the kids'll be getting Christmas presents this year."

HORSE FLU: THE TRAIL OF EQUINE DEVASTATION

Equine influenza crashed into Australia's racing industry and caused a sniffly, sore throated ruckus. In the wake of the epidemic, life has become very difficult for riders, trainers and owners...not to mention the afflicted horses themselves. In fact, since the first case was recorded earlier this year:

- Sales of equine Dimetapp, Vicks Hay Drops and giant tissues have skyrocketed.

- Bart Cummings has hocked his Golden Slippers and started selling *Big Issue* to make ends meet.

- Jockeys have been forced to take up humiliating positions in Wizard Of Oz stageshows and those TV ads where it's really funny because they've been given deep voices.

- Trainers have experimented with teaching other animals to race – so far they've had no luck fitting wombats or kangaroos with saddles, but the emus could be a goer.

- Some affected horses have become depressed, leading them to dye their manes black, comb them into a side fringe and start listening to My Chemical Romance.

- Angry tween girls have been ritually burning their *Saddle Club* DVDs.

- Johnny Tapp has released an album of his greatest calls to raise money for destitute racing identities.

CELEBRITY DEATHS

Who's next?

Steve Irwin and Peter Brock died last year. At the time, everyone was saying "bad things come in threes", conveniently ignoring the timely death of author Colin Thiele, overlooked in favour of someone more suited to a belated Channel 9 tribute special. Don Chipp doesn't count either – Irwin and Brock's companion has to be an Aussie hero cut down in their prime, doing what they loved. That way Karl Stefanovic can coax sound bites from devastated yet stalwart friends, family and ex-wives. To this end, I'd like to put forward a few potential candidates for the Australian Icon Trifecta.

Bert Newton

Probable cause: Poisoned by arsenic in his face make-up

Channel 9 will be able to run a full-blown special on Bert, detailing his rise to fame, early vaudeville work with Graham Kennedy and a very special *20 to 1* featuring his funniest televisual moments. It could be hosted by an obviously distraught Patti and his "actor" son Matthew.

Laurie Lawrence

Probable Cause: Embolism during high-octane motivational speech

There would be plenty of Australian and international athletes prepared to go on record as considering Laurie to be a top bloke. The number of hilarious anecdotes attributable to him would allow Channel 9 to do a whole month of tribute shows. Be prepared for plenty of slow-motion footage of Laurie celebrating Olympic wins in a flamboyant and jubilant style.

Ray Martin

Probable Cause: Murdered by shonky businessman in a "best served cold" revenge killing

Ray's move from serious *60 Minutes* journalism to *A Current Affair* beat-ups could be lovingly chronicled by a team of respectful Aussie journalists like Mike Munro, Jana Wendt and Mike Willesee. Bucketloads of funny and touching footage from *The Midday Show* could be shown, along with special remembrances from Kerri-Anne Kennerley, Rob Sitch and Eric Bana.

Paul Hogan

Probable Cause: Accidentally stabbed by Michael Caton during filming of *Crocodile Dundee 4: Stranger Bedfellows*

In a "That's Not a Legend, *This* Is a Legend" special, Channel 9 could show all his movies, from *Crocodile Dundee* to *Flipper* and beyond. Or more accurately, below. Of course, there'd be plenty of irreverence as the nation once again enjoyed Paul's unique brand of "fish out of water" humour from the 1970s with reruns of *The Paul Hogan Show* running through the month. In America, there would be hundreds of "shrimp on the barbie" references by lazy night-show hosts.

Bindi Irwin

Probable Cause: Wanting to be just like her Dad

Think endless repeats of that poxy new *Jungle Girl* series, and lots of moving interviews with the Crocmen. And of course even more merchandise than she produces already. What's more, just as Bindi came to the world's attention during a touching eulogy, her funeral could be the perfect opportunity for Baby Bob to take on the mantle as the next true successor of the Crocodile Hunter.

Homeless community agrees to phase out giant plastic bag usage

Many homeless people are switching to reusable bags and trolleys

In what has been described as a massive coup for Australia's environmental movement, the nation's homeless have put their support behind the push to phase out giant plastic bags. "This is a great day for Mother Nature," said Clean Up Australia spokesman Ian Kiernan. "From now on, we can expect to see homeless people using reusable giant green bags to carry their meagre possessions, not those planet-harming stripey plastics."

Although they were slow to mobilise, the homeless community's response was overwhelming. "When I overheard two businessmen talking about global warming while they pretended I didn't exist, I knew something had to be done," said Mary Hood, of No Fixed Abode. "And if that means filling my shabby shopping trolley with fewer plastic bags, then that's a sacrifice I'm willing to make on behalf of planet Earth."

"Think globally, act locally," she added, rummaging in a bin for reusable food and drink containers.

Fellow long-term vagrant Dave Whittaker agrees: "When you sleep outside with only a threadbare blanket and the day's newspapers to keep you warm, you really notice the effects of climate change. That's why I'm campaigning for the *Sydney Morning Herald* and *Australian* to be printed on 100% recycled paper. I'll sleep soundly knowing that my bedsheets are not contributing to deforestation," he said.

"Actually I'll sleep soundly anyway, in my usual meths-induced stupor," he added. "But you know what I mean."

Other hobo initiatives include recycling cigarettes, cleaning commuters' windscreens with biodegradable sponges and a number of water-saving programs. "Everyone can cut down," explained tone-deaf busker Jared Stephenson. "With our country in a drought, it's irresponsible to shower every day. And why waste water on flushing toilets when you can just as easily urinate in an alley?"

Australians have been asked to thank the homeless by giving them their unwanted metal coins for recycling into alcoholic beverages.

the joy of moving

Whether you're taking your first awkward steps from the family nest and into a sharehouse, intending to cohabit with the love of your life or slinking into a one-bedroom flat once that joyous relationship comes to a screaming halt, moving is a torturous and evil process that causes nothing but grief and heartache.

Finding a place

The first thing you will need to do is determine what kind of abode you would like to inhabit. Are you looking for a massive harbourside mansion with your one true love? If so, fuck you. Everyone else who's going to be going it alone or sharing on a temporary basis, listen up. There are a number of roads you can go down here, but only two of them are acceptable options. Basically, your choice is going to be between Expensive Apartment or Relatively Cheap Hovel.

EXPENSIVE APARTMENT: This security-building, city-views flat with two showers, three toilets and a massive entertainment area would be the envy of your friends, if you could afford to have any. Over 75% of your weekly income will go on rent, and every waking moment will be spent fielding calls from the owner about excess water usage, how many people are allowed to visit at a time and why the windows weren't properly cleaned last time they drove past.

RELATIVELY CHEAP HOVEL: Sure, rats might run across your doona all night, you'll be picking cockroaches out of your morning coffee and listening to your neighbours fucking through the wafer-thin walls all night, but at least you can afford to go out, right? Well – you could go out, if you were willing to leave your possessions unguarded against the army of ice addicts waiting outside to steal and hock them.

Packing

It's only when you come to the point where you have to put all of your possessions into cardboard boxes that you truly realise how much useless shit humans accumulate in their day-to-day dealings with the world. When all is said and done, you will vow never to let your hoard of stuff get so out of hand again, only to go through the exact same process next time you move. The only saving grace next time will be the discovery of unpacked boxes of books and knick-knacks, gathering dust as they patiently wait to be shifted to your next abode.

Removalists

Not to speak in generalities, but every single removalist is a grasping, money-hungry bastard who will underquote by at least 50%. Even worse, because they spend their days lugging heavy furniture from place to place, they're all built like brick shithouses, which makes arguing over the bill a daunting prospect at best. If you can con your friends and family into helping you lift revoltingly weighty boxes into a hired truck, go for it. Otherwise, brace yourself. It's gonna hurt.

Real estate

If you thought the removalists were bad, wait until you meet the real estate. They're just as evil, but they stay with you *forever*. I'm talking about tenancy here, where there are countless inspections, accusations of harbouring pets, rent hikes, "friendly" letters that try to make their employees look like a happy family of nice people and – worst of all – their constant lies about the qualities of any house or flat in their portfolio. Also, if a decent place *does* happen to become available, be prepared for shameless deposit auctions.

All you'll be able to afford. Described in the ad as "4 bed 2 bath charming residence with oodles of character"

If you own your home, then you only have to deal with the real estate when you're buying or selling. Good for you, mortgage monkey. Good for you.

The bond

Just when you've budgeted everything out and are ready to jump from one place to the other, you'll remember that a large chunk of money is yet to be removed from your bank account. Even if you've rented before, you probably lost your previous bond because of the time your cat or drunk cousin pissed on the carpet. Or you got it back and immediately spent it all on pizza, top-shelf whiskey and novelty shoes.

Meeting the neighbours

Doesn't happen. All your interaction will take place through the medium of terse notes slid under doors, or through the police. Especially if you wear an iPod every time you leave the house.

Final word

The best advice anyone can give when it comes to moving is to put it off for as long as possible. Cling to your current living situation like it was the last shred of hope in an otherwise meaningless existence. And if you absolutely, positively have to move house, try to con your parents, friends or flatmates into doing most of the work. Faking an injury's a good way to get out of heavy lifting, and grandparents are always good people to bite for the bond. If all else fails and your move turns out to have been foolish, don't worry – you can always just go through the exorbitant agony of moving house all over again.

In real life, as opposed to clip art, packing is rarely this fun, organised or picturesquely multiracial

Interest in disfigured child's brave struggle entirely due to grossout factor

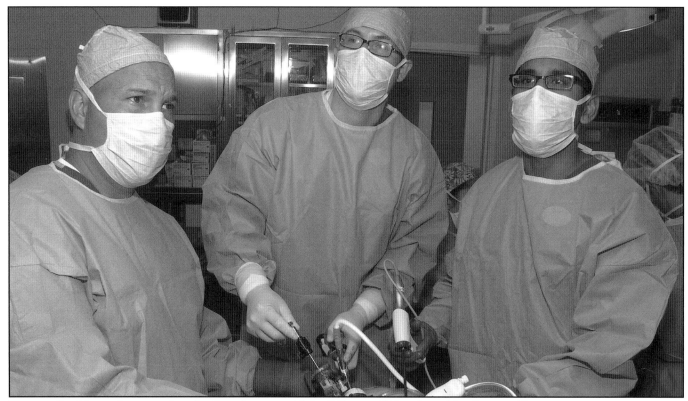

The surgical team in a passionate dispute over which of them will by played by George Clooney

With one swift sweep of a scalpel, Korean surgeons began a 14-hour operation on Tuesday to save a very special boy whose plight has come to captivate the nation. At only four years of age, Ko Jae-Sung has become a national hero, enduring scores of hours of surgery in his short life in an attempt to correct a rare genetic disorder which has left him with a massive, gross, purple freak head.

Hunter Dodson, the world-renowned craniofacial surgeon flown into Seoul for the landmark surgical intervention, hopes the decision to televise Ko Jae-Sung's operation live across the nation will bring greater public understanding of recent advances in the treatment of severe fibrous dysplasia when suffered in conjunction with never-before-seen extremes of neurofibromatosis. "People are going to be real surprised by what is possible these days in craniofacial surgery," Mr Dodson said. "Once we dig in, hack off all those disgusting dangly bits of his face and stitch everything up, I predict a sharp funding increase."

"I admire this boy for his great stoicism," said a local soft drink vendor. "His determination brings great honour to our country and the video of the actual operation, as well as being educational, is pretty fucking full-on. I mean, it's like a massive tumour – it must weigh a good six or seven kilos."

On a popular breakfast television chat show, Jae-Sung's parents have endured unusually pointed questioning. Father JaeJoong, a respected member of the renowned Zaytun Division of the Republic of Korea Army, was asked how he might feel if his son died on the operating table in this most precarious of operations, an operation beamed by satellite to hundreds of thousands of viewers in this country, and perhaps millions beyond its borders. "We are philosophical," he said. "For us, Jae-Sung is a blessing. The country has shared in his life and we believe that if the country is there in his most difficult moment, his triumph is more likely."

But outside the studio, the sentiments were different. "It is time to face that the death of Jae-Sung on the operating theatre is now a real possibility," said an early morning commuter. "With that possibility comes the realisation that we could watch the boy die, right in front of our eyes, on television. It'd be a total freak-out. I'm definitely watching."

Whatever happens to Jae-Sung, he won't soon be forgotten. The international rights to footage of his operation has already been sold to *Gross Out VI: Shit You Won't Believe They Caught On Tape.*

An open letter to Ms Kate Middleton from Mr Harry M. Miller

Dear Kate,

Once upon a time, there was a girl named Kate, and she met the man of pretty much every girl's dreams. He was blond, tall, a bit handsome, rich, splendidly posh and he could have made her a queen, had they managed to get married and live happily ever after. But they didn't, did they, Kate? So what are you going to do now?

Now, I know what you're thinking right now. You're thinking that the most important thing is to be dignified, stay out of the papers and generally keep a stiff upper lip.

That's absolutely the right thing to do. I mean, if I were your publicist, God forbid, I wouldn't hear of you doing anything else. Abso-positive-lutely not. No, ma'am. (Actually, they won't call you ma'am anymore, will they? Oh, sorry, that's a touch insensitive, isn't it? Bit of a raw nerve there? Have a tissue, love. More champagne?)

But ... that doesn't preclude just working through a few ideas, you know, hypothetically, does it? Have you fully considered all of your options, professionally speaking? Because it looks to me like stony silence in the face of the on-coming media circus is not only less than optimal, commercially-speaking, but also a bit unfair. Even a bit selfish.

Why would I say unfair? Well, it just seems to me that Wills would want you to at least have a chance to explain your side of things to the world, wouldn't he? After all, what sort of unchivalrous cad would ask a girl to put up with all this and never strike back? I mean, it isn't as he's there to face the press with you any more now, is it? (Oh God, there I go again, me and my big mouth, dry those eyes, love, I'm sorry – top up your glass?)

The good news is this: my name is Harry, and it is my job to know exactly how to help people like you, who find themselves in a tricky spot over a bit of media coverage. Clearly, any kind of exploitation of your newly vulnerable state is off-limits - I am bound by strict publicist's ethics, after all – so this advice is coming to you absolutely gratis.

But I couldn't help but notice that Prince William's picture was in the papers today. And he was smiling. So someone looks like they're moving on, wouldn't you say?

So here's what you do. Don't worry about him. He'll be fine. He's got the weight of the monarchy to sustain him in the difficult days ahead. Army, shmarmy – the biggest risk to William's health is that he gets hit by an avalanche of frenzied gold-digging blue-bloods the next time he steps foot inside a London nightclub. Although to be fair, it is a real risk.

(Now, I appreciate that this may seem like an odd question, but do you happen to have, say, a few souvenirs left from your royal encounters? Say, a few saucy pictures taken on your mobile phone perhaps? Or even a semen-spattered dress? You never know when these things might come in handy.)

Where was I? Oh yes: doing the right thing. Very important. But what is it? My professional opinion is this: there is only one truly noble and selfless act left for you to undertake. Sell the lot. You must get your story out there.

After all, it was Buckingham Palace themselves that made the original announcement, wasn't it? Think about it for a moment. All you'd do is help them out, by filling some gaps left in the story. It's what the royal family would want you to do, I think. Certainly it's what Diana would want you to do. She's was the People's Princess: wouldn't she want her people to hear about her boy? I'm sure she would. And have you considered how proud she would be if you sang his praises on *Celebrity Love Island*?

Now you might think that some details are too intimate to be laid out raw in the media for everyone to dissect. I hear you. But neither of us are really in a position to judge that, are we? So the only fair, truly fair, way to deal with that question is to expose it all, and then let people decide what's important and what is not. In, ahem, the marketplace of ideas.

You don't have to reveal everything, of course. Not at all. If I were to book you a photoshoot with, let's say, *FHM* – in the best possible taste, of course – you would be more than welcome to leave your bikini on. At least, in most of the shots.

But Kate, it's not just about you, and your grief. This is no time to think of yourself. The people must know. They have a right to know. They must know about their future king. Where you went, what you did and how many times you did it. His thoughts, his foibles, his drunken bouts of inconsiderate love-making, his likely actions in a constitutional crisis, his pet names for his penis. (Little Willy, perhaps?) Every detail counts. It is a matter of the public interest, you understand.

I'm waiting for your call.

Yours sincerely

Harry M. Miller